THE
MAGIC

and

MAYHEM
OF
DONALD
TRUMP

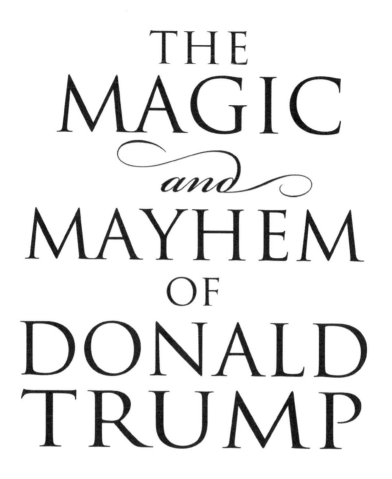

THE MAGIC *and* MAYHEM OF DONALD TRUMP

A STRATEGIC EXCERPT OF
BORN TO FIGHT: LINCOLN & TRUMP

GRETCHEN WOLLERT

PLAIN SIGHT PUBLISHING
An imprint of Cedar Fort, Inc.
Springville, Utah

Paperback ISBN 13: 978-1-4621-4860-8
eBook ISBN 13: 978-1-4621-4861-5

Published by Cedar Fort Publishing & Media, Inc.
2373 W. 700 S., Suite 100 Springville, UT 84663
Distributed by Cedar Fort, Inc., www.cedarfort.com

Library of Congress Control Number: 2024942451

Cover design by Shawnda Craig
Cover design © 2024 Cedar Fort, Inc.
Edited and Typeset by Evelyn Coleman

Printed in the United States of America

10 9 8 7 6 5 4 3 2 1

Printed on acid-free paper

Contents

Preface

Too young to vote as a junior in high school, yet fascinated with her online American history course, my third daughter, Gabrielle, felt convicted to call leadership to action the way the great leaders of America's past once did. That year, she competed against students from allover the nation in Public Speaking II at the Future Business Leaders of America's National Leadership Conference. In her short five-minute speech, she condensed months of preparation,captivated a room of her peers, and defined what makes great leaders. That she won the competition—giving the best of the best speech of that year, 2014—showcased not just her skill in the delivery, but also revealed a significant relevance in her message. Some of America's most visible and vocal national leaders at the time seemed to be doing more apologizing for America's history than learning from it. A year later a most unusual candidate would throw his hat into the presidential ring, challenge a mediocre status quo by doing so, and turn American politics on its head for years to come. This was her speech:

Five were captured and imprisoned as traitors; Twelve had their homes ransacked and burned; Nine fought and died from wounds and hardships of the war. Fifty-six men pledged their lives, fortunes and sacred honor by signing their names to the Declaration of Independence. Their signature was a death warrant, and they knew it.

This was a time for greatness. And these were ordinary men who lived ordinary lives until faced with a cause that was much greater than themselves. How many of us today know what it means to stand firm for such a cause? Who are the leaders to inspire us to action and help us stand taller?

There was a time in history when the words of great leaders raised us up and moved us to want to do great things. Where are these leaders? We are these leaders. As Future Business Leaders of America it is up to us to develop character, prepare for useful citizenship, and foster patriotism.

Great leaders have conviction, a fire within—a passion for the cause. As Benjamin Franklin stated when signing his own name to the Declaration, 'We must all hang together or assuredly we shall all hang separately.' They were committed and were unified. We must lead with conviction and spirit.

Great leadership is not defined by short bursts of emotion but by the sincere dedication of a lifetime. Thomas Jefferson, when drafting the Declaration of Independence, was not just declaring independence but creating a representation of what America was to become—a great nation. And as future leaders of such it is our responsibility to remember and preserve these examples from our past.

Our future as leaders depends on our ability to develop character. Character is knowing the difference between what is right and what is wrong and having the courage to do what is right. America was founded on principles, and these principles must be found in the hearts of its people. Who better to inspire us today to be virtuous but leaders with genuine character and honest in what they say and do.

George Washington was a perfect example of this. Following the Revolutionary War Congress didn't have enough funds to pay the soldiers for their service. This caused outrage and discontent among the ranks. Washington, in a final attempt to calm them, began reading a letter from Congress—he then stopped. He reached into his pocket and pulled out something these men had never seen him use before—his spectacles.

'Gentlemen,' he said quietly, 'You must pardon me. I have grown gray in your service and now find myself growing blind.' This honest, humble act moved these men to set aside their discontent. We as future leaders must learn to lead not only with words, but with simple, genuine actions.

Thomas Paine in 1776 wrote, 'These are the times that try men's souls. The summer soldier and sunshine patriot will shrink from the service of this country.' Our founders were simple, ordinary people like you and me, but they had courage. They did not shrink from challenge. Patrick Henry, when debating between freedom or security declared 'Give me liberty or give me death.' Now that is courage—the kind of courage leaders today must have when facing challenges.

Theodore Roosevelt once said 'No man is worth his salt who is not ready at all times to risk . . . his life in a great cause.' Our great cause is a war against indifference—indifference to mediocrity in the workplace and the world.

Our founders' love for this country was deep and intense. On Independence Day, they laid it all on the line. As the future of this nation, we should look to the examples of our past. We are provided the opportunity to be great leaders, to develop character, become people of virtue, and share a love for our country just as our first leaders had.

When you look to our flag—a representation of our nation and its principles—remember the truths of our nation's past. Those who fought for it were not giants. They were ordinary people like you and like me who chose to overcome mediocrity and rise above their own insecurities to change the world.

Gabrielle Wollert,
2014 FBLA National
Leadership Conference,
Public Speaking II
1st Place

Chapter One
An American Tale

"Let him run; there's time enough yet for him to learn his letters and get pokey.
Bob was just such a little rascal, and now he is a very decent boy."

-Abraham Lincoln to Noah Brooks on his sons (no date)

BEFORE THERE WAS A DONALD TRUMP, THERE WAS A FRED TRUMP; AND before there was a Fred Trump, there was Friedrich Trump: Donald's paternal grandfather—a man Donald never knew or saw.

Friedrich was born and raised in Germany, all the way up to his sixteenth year of life before he bolted in a fit of youthful adventure for a faraway land. He had grown up in the village of Kallstadt in southwestern Germany, in a region known as Pfalz, described a century later as a lush, pleasant, and affluent place,[1] but which those many decades earlier was a disturbing place for a restless lad with lofty ambitions, offering nothing of note for young Friedrich.

No question; he wanted out of Pfalz, a region nestled in the foothills of the Haardt Mountains. Shunning a military service obligation that was to soon kick in for him, sixteen-year-old Friedrich set off, alone, for America in October 1885. In running away from home, he boldly abandoned his family and an inheritance that had become so small as to be almost useless. (Germany's mandated apportionment laws introduced almost a century earlier by Napoleon meant family lands were divided up equally among offspring.) There was little to tempt him to stay. Instead, he was determined to seek success and fortune in the United States, his intent to become wealthy with haste by brandishing the grit and tenacity that would become a Trump trademark.

Friedrich didn't cross the Atlantic, destination New York, without having a trade skill in hand. Back in Germany, he had served an apprenticeship for about two and a half years as a barber, cutting hair. He also wasn't entirely alone when he got to America. His older sister, Katharina, had immigrated to New York several years earlier and was now living with her husband Fred Schuster on Manhattan's Lower East Side, in a neighborhood of numerous Palatine German immigrants.

Good fortune sometimes comes to the bold. As fate would have it, young Friedrich quickly met a German-speaking barber who was looking for someone immediately available to take on an assistant's role. For the next six years he worked as a barber, all the while knowing this wasn't going to be his life's work. It certainly wasn't an occupation that would bring wealth quickly—by the time nine years had passed, he had merely several hundred dollars to his name accompanied by an itch to get to work for real, and, in his case, to move on to greener pastures.

And what a move it was—completely across the country. Friedrich Trump left Manhattan in 1891 and headed west to Seattle, where he used his modest life savings to buy a restaurant in the city's red-light district, which he furnished with new tables, chairs, and a range. He excelled at serving the public and assured patrons a good meal, a stiff drink, and even more recreational pursuits.

For the next ten years, Friedrich Trump—by now better known as "Frederick" Trump—bounced around the Pacific Northwest, leaving Seattle after three years. In British Columbia and the Yukon he rubbed elbows with miners while still making a go of it in the hotel and restaurant business. Eventually, he and a business partner founded the Arctic Restaurant and Hotel in Bennett, British Columbia. Then two years later, in 1900, they launched the Yukon-based White Horse Restaurant and Inn. It proved to be a huge financial success, serving three thousand meals a day with plenty of space available to feed one's taste for gambling. A year later, Trump sold his share in the business to his partner and headed back to Germany as a somewhat wealthy man.[2]

Back home in Kallstadt, Frederick wasted no time in finding a wife, marrying Elisabeth Christ, eleven years his junior, before moving to New York City in 1902. Elisabeth's homesickness made it a brief stay in America, less than two years. Before leaving the U.S., however, Elisabeth gave birth to their daughter Elizabeth in April 1904. A few months later, they were headed back to Germany. That, too, would be a short stay. Bavarian authorities finally caught up with Friedrich's years-earlier avoidance of military service when he had first fled to America, now labeling him a draft dodger.

A royal decree issued In February 1905 informed Trump that he had eight weeks to get out of the country for not having properly registered his 1886 departure with authorities. He put his wife Elisabeth and baby on a boat and headed back to America for good. That summer of 1905 their first son, Fred (Donald Trump's father-to-be) was born.

Having invested in land in the Pacific Northwest about a decade earlier, Frederick wasted little time in buying another chunk of real estate. In 1908, he purchased property on Jamaica Avenue in the Woodhaven area of Queens, New York. Two years later, he moved his family there and rented out rooms in the spacious residence, helping to defray some of the family's living expenses. As he was starting to build his real estate portfolio, Frederick Trump was also working as a hotel manager at a property at 6th Avenue and 23rd Street.

Still in his early forties at the time, Frederick was finally able to enjoy the modest wealth he had accumulated (equivalent to a little over a half million dollars in today's currency), with designs to further expand his investments into land. What he hadn't planned for was an early death. It was on a Wednesday near the end of May 1918, on the eve of Memorial Day, when Frederick Trump and young Fred, twelve at the time, were walking along Jamaica Avenue. They often did this in the afternoon, dropping in to chat with realtors along the way. At some point Frederick suddenly turned to his son, saying he felt sick. They hastened home, where the elder Trump immediately crawled into bed and then died within hours, "just like that," in the words of young Fred, recalling the event years later.[3]

Frederick Trump was forty-nine years old when he died. The cause— Spanish flu. Five days later, his brother-in-law, Fred Shuster, passed away, also a Spanish flu victim, putting them among the tens of millions of people worldwide who eventually died from one of the deadliest epidemics of the twentieth century.[4]

Believe it or not, Donald Trump doesn't relish answering questions about himself, his upbringing, or his ancestry. Trump says that people who watched him on The Apprentice, read his books, or attended his Learning Annex seminars might think they know him, but they know only part of him—his business side. "I usually don't speak much about . . . my personal values or about how I came to be who I am today," he points out.[5] In his autobiography The Art of the Deal he writes, "Contrary to what a lot of people think, . . . I don't particularly like talking about my personal life."[6]

In one account of Trump's ancestry the story of an immigrant leaving the homeland for new and wider horizons in America did not necessarily foster pride immediately in the family.

Fred Trump, Donald's father, who was forty-one years Donald's senior, had concerns about his family's heritage. Fred was described as self-conscious, perhaps even ashamed, of his German lineage, instead telling people that he was Swedish—that his father, Friedrich, had come to the United States from Sweden and not Germany, a claim Donald Trump repeated in his earliest book.[7]

Friedrich, nonetheless—country of origin aside—left a legacy that included boldness and a stubborn tenacity apparent in the Trump family line. His son Fred was described as a man of grit, someone who embodied discipline, consistency, and a determination to get the job done right. If it wasn't right, he would make sure it got fixed, often taking care of it himself. He was not one to give up easily on a matter, even when friends and colleagues suggested to him that he take another course of action–a quality of stubbornness often associated with Donald. About Fred Trump, attorney Sydney Young once said, "You could never tell Fred Trump what to do. You could tell him how to do it, but not what to do. He was very strong-willed."[8]

Fred Trump made it a point to know what was going on in the world around him, especially when it might involve business matters. Following in his own father's business footsteps, Fred discovered something in the mid-1930s that would provide a sustained lifeblood of opportunities in the construction business. At the time, Fred was hitting his thirties and Donald was still ten years away from being born. His newfound ticket to business success: the government.

Thanks to a number of New Deal programs pushed into existence by President Franklin D. Roosevelt's administration, new heavily financed opportunities were being offered to help float businesses such as Fred's. He proved skilled at determining how to take full advantage of these programs. In so doing, Fred Trump "joined the ranks of entrepreneurs who constitute one of the oldest fraternities in the Republic: multimillionaires who owe their fortune to subsidies from a grateful government."[9] Donald learned early that using the system to full advantage would serve him at times in climbing his own ladder of success.

Life inside the Trump home on Midland Parkway in Queens was caring but strict, complete with rules and curfews. For Donald's sister, Maryanne, that meant no lipstick. Sweets and snacks between meals were not allowed, and when Fred, the dad (there was also a Fred Jr., Donald's older brother) came home from work at night, Mom would dutifully inform her husband about what the kids had done that day and how they had behaved. Then he would mete out whatever punishments were called for. "Spare the rod, spoil the child."

All five of the Trump children—Maryanne, Fred Jr., Elizabeth, Donald, and Robert—were taught to be frugal and respect the value of a dollar. That meant turning out all the lights in rooms not being used, cleaning their plates at every meal, and being aware and attentive to starving children around the world. Each of them worked summer jobs, which for the three boys included paper routes; their only concession being that when it rained or snowed, they could use the limousine to get to all of their delivery destinations. "The first time I ever realized that my father was successful," Maryanne said," was when I was fifteen and a friend said to me, 'Your father is rich.' I was stunned. We were privileged, but I didn't know it."[10]

Donald may seem a poster child for "excess," but frugality was actually a hallmark of the Trump household. His father, Fred, had few peers when it came to his version of frugality and being a model caretaker of finances and goods. There are many stories about his penny-pinching, such as picking up stray nails at a job site and returning them to the workers the next day— simultaneously saving money and setting an example for his son Donald. To cut down on supply costs, he had chemists research the formula for the floor disinfectant he purchased in large quantities. Then had workers mix up batches of the disinfectant at a cost significantly less than what he had been paying to a vendor. If he felt there were any lights that could be turned off without affecting the overall lighting, he would think nothing of getting up on a stepladder and removing any light bulbs he thought were unnecessary.[11] How many Trumps did it take to change a light bulb? One, apparently.

Fred would tell young Donald, "The most important thing in life is to love what you're doing, because that's the only way you'll ever be really good at it."[12] And Fred loved to work! He typically worked twelve-hour workdays (also known as "half-days" to the world's most devoted workaholics), sometimes busting it right alongside his construction workers. On exceptionally busy days he would come home after fourteen hours and then sit in his library answering telephone calls for another hour or two. "My work ethic came from my father," Donald said. "I don't know anybody who works harder than I do. I'm working all the time. It's not about money—I just don't know a different way of life, and I love it."[13]

It was that Trump nose for business and Fred Trump's business acumen and ambition that set them apart. By age twenty-one, Fred Trump was already diving headfirst into New York City real estate, joining forces with his mother Elisabeth in doing business with E. Trump and Son. Where Donald and his father veered sharply was a penchant for playing it safe when it came to business. Fred Trump and his mother Elisabeth chose the outer boroughs of Brooklyn and Queens for their business ventures rather than fighting it out with cutthroat developers in the fierce (and expensive!) competitive fires of Manhattan.[14] "The real reason I wanted out of my father's business," Donald wrote in his autobiography *The Art of the Deal*, "was that I had loftier dreams and visions. And there was no way to implement them building housing in the outer boroughs."[15]

Donald admits his dad's business was a little too physically rough for his liking.[16] Many times when Fred went to collect rent from tenants in tough sections of Brooklyn, he would bring young Donald along, as much to learn the business as to be exposed to seedier parts of the city he otherwise would not have cause to visit. At times, Donald watched his dad ring the doorbell at a tenant's residence then stand off to the side of the door, knowing an angry tenant might shoot through the door in lieu of paying rent.[17]

His father Fred's confident persona in the world of business and construction unnerved competitors, but not his son. Donald Trump wasn't intimidated by his dad and had no fear of standing up to him because younger Trump said so: "Fortunately for me, I was drawn to business very early, and I was never intimidated by my father, the way most people were. I stood up to him, and he respected that. We had a relationship that was almost businesslike. I sometimes wonder if we'd have gotten along so well if I hadn't been as business-oriented as I am."[18]

Fred didn't always click with Donald when it came to business matters, but he respected his son's robust work ethic and his knack for producing great results. Looking back in his 2015 book *Great Again*, Trump related, "I took what I learned from my father and built my own business—and no one was more proud of me than my father." At one point Fred told a business magazine, "Everything Donald touches turns to gold!"[19] There were also those times when a proud papa would pull out a photo of Donald in a tuxedo and show it around. Sometimes his audience would already know who the young Trump was, a sure sign of the impact Donald was making in the business world at an early age.

While Trump grew up surrounded by his father's wealth, little was given to Donald during his schooling years. He was put to work, and it was hard work, with long hours; there was no coasting for anything work-related for the five Trump siblings. Trump's mother, Mary Anne (MacLeod), was part of that hard-work ethic as well, working full-time in various ways alongside her husband and children. One way was collecting all the change from the coin-operated laundry machines in all the Trump real-estate developments.

Fulfilling considerable ambitions of her own, including being the matriarch of the home, was a real determinative connection to her son. She had been adventurous and secure enough in herself to leave her home in a distant country, marry a husband and establish her own home in a far-away place. She nurtured her children, filling her home with love, civility and care. But she also prodded her children to follow pursuits of self-betterment, to be all they could be. "My mother was the perfect housewife," Donald explained, "There were five children in all and besides taking care of us, she cooked and cleaned and darned socks and did charity work at the local hospital."[20]

Donald's relationship with his mother involved a shared competitive streak, a virtue when it came to dealing with the vagaries of the competitive business in which they worked alongside Fred—real estate. "My mother was silently competitive," Donald also said, long after she had passed away at age 88 in 2000. "She was a very competitive person, but you wouldn't know that. She had a great fighting spirit, like Braveheart."[21] Indeed, Mrs. Trump had a strong bearing and confidence about her, a commanding feminine presence. She was energetic and strong-willed, a most impressive woman of her era, almost regal in countenance and appearance, influenced by the fact that she was tall and slender, and always well-dressed with a "crown" of impressively coiffed hair she wore much of her life. And she spoke with a slight Scottish brogue (she had been born in the Scottish village of Tong, closer to Iceland than London).[22]

Mary Anne McCleod Trump was definitely queen of her castle—a twenty-three room mansion (including nine bathrooms) with the utilitarian vibe of a builder instead of the grandiosity of an architect. Fred wasn't flashy. In his home he wanted practicality and efficiency, like built-in cabinets and an intercom system, not cathedral ceilings.[23] Mary Anne made it useful and modern, and she made sure it was ruled by order, competence, and as much added elegance as she could muster. Donald described her in his autobiography, *The Art of the Deal*, as someone who loved splendor and magnificence, a trait that influenced his own sense of style and showmanship. "She always had a flair for the dramatic and the grand," he added.[24]

There are two things Donald Trump seems to value more than anything else when he speaks of his own upbringing. One is "the best 'genes' that anybody could get," his lock into what he called "the lucky sperm club."[25] The other is the Bible given to him by his mother upon his confirmation as a boy. Trump admits showing it often during the 2016 presidential campaign to groups of potential voters when sharing about his mother or his faith.

Over the years, Trump has been given hundreds of Bibles by admirers. But the one that connects him to his mother, he counts as most special. "I was sworn in on the very Bible from which my mother would teach us as young children," Trump shared in February 2017 at the National Prayer Breakfast.[26] But it was more than just a visual aid at campaign events. When facing a critical gathering of wary faith leaders from the African-American community in 2015, he entered the meeting holding the Bible out in front of him, then confessed with a smile, "Most of the time I bring this Bible as a prop when I'm sharing about my mother . . . In this case, I'm simply holding it for protection."[27]—like a shield on the field of battle.

Chapter Two
Simple Faith

"I have often wished that I was a more devout man than I am."

-Abraham Lincoln to the Baltimore Presbyterian
Synod, Oct. 24, 1863

MANY MIGHT DISMISS AS INCONCEIVABLE ANY SUGGESTION THAT Donald Trump believed in a power higher than himself. Through the eighties it seemed every other tabloid front-page story about Trump proclaimed yet another outlandish worldly episode in the ongoing saga of his self-serving, lavish, and dissipated lifestyle. How could a person portrayed in the media as such a "bad boy" be a person of faith? When judging Trump by only what is seen and heard in the news, he had no "Christian character" or any kind of "redemptive nature." But what was apparent on the surface belied a depth of faith not readily seen by outsiders.

Donald Trump was the pompous billionaire with the jumbo-sized ego, three times married, at least four businesses bankrupted (six if you are to believe Hillary Clinton), one alleged affair with a porn actress, caught on tape spewing crude locker-room bluster, and offender to millions of Americans unaccustomed to reading a president's unfiltered (yet brutally honest and oftentimes spot-on) social media posts that violate codes of PC conduct embraced by the truly enlightened.

Considering all that, it's no wonder that Trump has never been treated by contemporary media as a man of particularly robust religious faith or expression. The remarkable truth is that he is a man of faith, even if not in the eyes of his judgmental critics.

When it comes to demonstrations of a belief in God, prayer, worship, and scripture, among Christians at least, judgmental churchgoers keep a hopeful eye out for stereotypes with a knack for quoting pet scriptural verses on cue, toting a Bible, and especially emoting during church worship, while perched in a pew every Sunday and other church holidays.

Trump isn't much for checking off any of those boxes. However, before we condemn him to an eternity in purgatory, let's remember that the Bible speaks openly of man's sinful nature and the hope for forgiveness available to any man or woman, boy or girl, who seeks a path to God, accompanied by sincere repentance. Trump is afforded that same opportunity.

What exactly does a man or woman have to do to convince family, friends, acquaintances, co-workers, and the public in general they are people of faith submitted to God? Actually, nothing. It's between them and God; no one else is qualified to make that judgment, despite what they see, hear, or read (or don't see, hear, or read). Trump has a foundation of faith that dates back to his youth. He grew up in a family that honored the Sabbath, the Bible, times of prayer, and church attendance. He learned about and (hopefully) followed the tenets of the Christian faith. We know of no evidence that Trump ever backed off or hid from his faith because a belief about a certain topic was "above his pay grade." At the National Prayer Breakfast in February of 2018 Trump revealed something about his personal faith, "I was blessed to be raised in a churched home. My mother and father taught me that to whom much is given much is expected . . . And that faith lives on in my heart every single day."[1]

Historical accounts about Trump's religious upbringing as a youth are scattered and relatively scant. One known fact is that his mother, Mary Anne, gave him his first Bible when he was eight years old—a Revised Standard Version (RSV) published by Thomas Nelson & Sons in 1952. The occasion, in June 1955, was Trump's graduation from Sunday Church Primary School at First Presbyterian Church (FPC) in his childhood neighborhood of Jamaica, Queens, New York.[2]

In the years since, the hundreds of Bibles gifted to him by admirers—many of whom were presumably concerned about Trump's relationship with God and his eternal destination—he says he has kept safely stowed away in a safe place in Trump Tower.[3]

"There's no way I would ever . . . do anything negative to a Bible . . . I would have a fear of doing something other than very positive," Trump said.[4]

Trump's childhood church is more than 350 years old and is currently tucked among chain stores, Bangladeshi food stands, and halal grocers in Jamaica, Queens. One ironic thing about the church and its connection to Trump is that it now boasts a congregation predominantly composed of immigrants from a dozen or more countries. On any given Sunday, as described in the July 2016 edition of The Atlantic, an attendee might see "women in geles and bright, African-print dresses (sitting) in the pews alongside ladies in floppy church hats."[5]

Although it was believed as of 2016 that Trump had not visited his childhood church in decades, he did send a $10,000 donation to FPC in 2012, according to Pastor Patrick O'Connor. "I attended Sunday school at the church for a number of years," Trump wrote. "Going to church was an important part of our family life, and the memories for me are still vivid— of a vibrant congregation and a lot of activities."[6]

Over the years, Trump has proudly recalled his confirmation into FPC in June 1959, the month in which he turned thirteen, on numerous occasions, often showing off a photo from the confirmation ceremony. Pictured are seven boys in the back row, most of them wearing dark suits—he's the tallest—with twelve girls in white dresses and flowers in the front two rows. Trump kept the photo handy during his 2016 presidential campaign, frequently pulling it out to show people as proof he had indeed been initiated into the folds of the church.

As part of the confirmation process, students were required to sign a document certifying they had "publicly confessed Jesus Christ as Lord and Savior and received into the communicant membership" of the local church. Included in that confirmation process was a service during which the nineteen students publicly confessed, confirmed, and promised to abide by several affirmations. It started with, "Do you confess your faith in God the Father Almighty, Maker of heaven and earth, and in Jesus Christ his only Son our Lord, and do you promise with the aid of the Holy Spirit to be Christ's faithful disciple to your life's end?"[7]

Whether Trump's profession of confirmation of an abiding faith and lifelong discipleship in Jesus Christ could be interpreted as a proclamation of being "born again" is debatable (once saved, always saved?). It seems reasonable to conclude, though, that Trump did successfully complete the confirmation process (perhaps considering it his first exclusive club membership). This process imbued him with a foundation of faith that has been with him his whole life, even if his words and actions haven't always passed muster with other believers—and, of course, nonbelievers.

Most Americans don't see Trump, who identifies as Presbyterian, as religious; half of them don't believe he is a Christian. Those were among the conclusions reached by a Pew Research Center survey conducted in early 2020. Announced March 25, 2020, Pew's survey results showed 63 percent of all U.S. adults claiming that Trump was either "not too" or "not at all" religious. There were 28 percent of respondents who said the forty-fifth U.S. president was "somewhat" religious, but only 7 percent stating he was "very" religious. Even among survey respondents identifying themselves as Christian, more than half doubted Trump's level of religious faith; 56 percent said he was "not too" or "not at all" religious, and 43 percent chose either "somewhat" or "very" as Trump's level of religiosity.[8]

Even though the Pew Research Center bills itself as "a nonpartisan fact tank that informs the public about the issues, attitudes, and trends shaping the world," its origins suggest otherwise. It was established so-named in 2004, with roots tracing back to the now-defunct Times Mirror Company. This company published newspapers (e.g., *Los Angeles Times, Newsday, Dallas Times Herald,* etc.) for more than a century, along with other print media.[9]

The Pew Center's survey findings make for interesting reading, especially for anti-Trumpers craving ammunition with which to launch yet another assault on Trump's character and fitness to lead the country. It's worth pointing out that in its lead paragraph on the story announcing its findings in this survey, the Center acknowledged that Trump's "personal religious beliefs and practices have not been as public as his penchant for surrounding himself with evangelical leaders while also supporting various conservative Christian causes, not to mention his frequent use of religious-oriented jargon while speaking in public."[10]

His detractors might claim that Trump's affinity for Christian language and advisors has essentially been a political strategy to endear himself to the Christian/evangelical voting bloc. But such an assumption falls short of properly evaluating Trump's private exercise of his Christian beliefs. While they are at it, his detractors might scrutinize and perhaps adjust their own beliefs and religious practices before ordaining themselves bully pulpit bishops, charged with deducing Trump's personal faith.

Membership in the club of presidents not known for their church attendance, and yet being open about staking the high ground on matters such as morals, conscience, and biblical principles, includes Abraham Lincoln, Dwight Eisenhower and Ronald Reagan. All were Republicans who regarded their respective eras' fight against Slavery/Communism as much a matter of morality as it was political, and all were not regular churchgoers.

Ditto for Donald Trump. But it is incorrect to label Trump as apathetic to religion and devoid of at least an appreciation and love for the teachings of Christ, just because he doesn't speak in tongues or memorize scriptural passages (as far as we know). A perceived lack of piety doesn't make him an atheist or agnostic.

Results of another survey conducted in November of 2023 asked over a thousand registered voters who they considered to be a person of faith among a list of current political figures. While Joe Biden was the top choice for Democrats, 64% of Republicans listed Donald Trump as a "person of faith"—beating out his more openly religious former vice president Mike Pence by a whopping eight points. Though the survey results showed a marked difference in the people's perception of "religious" versus "person of faith," the numbers clearly put Trump in the faithful category. Samuel Benson, national political correspondent for the Deseret News (the source for the survey), explains why:

> Those who said Trump was a person of faith or religious point to their perception of him as a defender of religious people or policies. Sixty-seven percent said Trump defends people of faith in the U.S.; 60% said he supports policies that focus on families; and 54% said he "cares about people like me."

> The least common reason for saying Trump is a person of faith or religious, expressed by only 26% of respondents, is that he is "actively involved in religious and faith communities."[11]

"In other words," writes Kelsey Dallas, assistant editor for the same news outlet, "these voters care more about his eagerness to appoint Supreme Court justices who oppose abortion or to design policies that protect faith groups that oppose same-sex marriage than his church attendance habits."[12]

Keep in mind, this survey occurred over two months after Trump's Fulton County, Georgia mug shot went viral on social media (over 287 million views on Trump's Twitter [X] account alone.) The intent of releasing the mug shot was meant to hurt Trump—his haters now had "proof" he was bad—right? But rather than hurt him, his supporters rallied around what they say was the injustice of it all. Not to mention, Trumpsters now had the ultimate fight poster, complete with piercing, angry eyes, and Trump's "let-me-at-him" look of a Buster Douglas ready to punch Mike Tyson's lights out. The arrest in August of 2023 was just the beginning of multiple indictments brought against Trump by Democrat district attorneys in Georgia, New York and Washington, D.C. Many Republicans called it politically motivated election interference meant to keep the former president from another White House run. Trump called it an outrageous "witch hunt."

Despite these legal battles, the numbers in this survey confirm Trump's perceived role as a "man of faith." Chalk it up to actions speaking louder than words, or possibly to something a young Trump learned from his mother's Bible teaching, that "a healthy tree bears good fruit."[13]

Donald's mother Mary Anne declared her commitment to the spiritual upbringing of her children when she said, "I tried to get it into their heads that they had to believe. Whether it shows or not, it's in there because I put it there."[14] Trump himself admits that his mother is the one who always said, "trust in God and be true to yourself."[15]

Other than Mary Anne, Trump's wife Melania, or any of his three adult children, the one person who knows the president's spiritual walk better than anybody else is Rev. Paula White-Cain, pastor of New Destiny Christian Center in Apopka, Florida, and chairwoman of Trump's first evangelical advisory board. At Trump's presidential inauguration on January 21, 2017, she became the first female clergyperson to speak at such an event. White's detractors point to her belief in the "prosperity gospel" as a sign that she wasn't an authentic Christian. Perhaps, the naysayers say, White was drawn to Trump because of his billions on paper, which in turn might have raised doubt about Trump's own authenticity when it came to religious matters. White is not shy about sticking up for Trump and his embrace of Christianity, the cynics be, well, darned.

As quoted from *The Faith of Donald J. Trump*, by David Brody and Scott Lamb:

> "The man that I know is a believer, a Christian, and a man that's hungry for God," White said, even if "he doesn't know our 'Christianese' and perhaps our language that we know in the Christian world."

As for the spiritual critics lined up at his door, White asked a very simple question: "If we just want to hold Mr. Trump to saying every day . . . he's going to be just spot on with God, well then I'd say, 'Are you?' No! None of us are. [The Apostle] Paul wasn't. The only one that was, was Jesus Christ."[16]

Trump has surrounded himself with Christian and evangelical leaders, which he started doing years before he announced for a presidential run in 2015. Still, without the Christian evangelical voter base behind him, he didn't stand a chance of winning in 2016. Evangelical leaders not already aligned to Trump the Man weren't going to hand Trump the Candidate their support and endorsements unless he came to them, which he did on September 29, 2016, in a private meeting at Trump Tower. There he gathered with a group of religious leaders that included Christian evangelicals and Catholics. Robert Jeffress, senior pastor of First Baptist Church in Dallas, mediated the meeting. "Many in that group were Never Trumpers, and you could tell they came ready to give him a piece of their mind that they probably couldn't afford to lose," Jeffress said later. "When he walked into the room, and I introduced them, he listened to them, he delayed his departure, and by the end of the meeting he had them eating out of the palm of his hand."[17]

Rev. Paula White-Cain, self-professed as having risen out of "trailer trash," wasn't among those Christian evangelical leaders who needed to be won over in 2016. She had already been there for him for more than ten years, since the first time he contacted her by phone after he saw her preach on TV in 2002.[18]

"Way before his run for the presidency, way before involvement in the (Republican) party, way before becoming a politician—he was a man seeking God," White said. "A man who was spiritually hungry, watching Christian television and listening to Southern Gospel music. We are this work in progress that is continually growing, as long as our heart is open to God and as long as we are seeking God."[19]

Another televangelist who has befriended Trump and served as a spiritual counselor for many years is Texas-based James Robison, who has said, "God uses imperfect people to accomplish his perfect will. He always has and always will."[20]

We all can probably agree that Donald Trump is less than perfect.

Trump rarely, if ever, attends church. And while Trump has been neglectful, if not dismissive, of the public side to his faith, he found that once he became president, he needed to be on the right side of a power much higher than his own. "I've always felt the need to pray," Trump said, "so I would say that the office is so powerful that you need God even more . . . there's almost not a decision that you make when you're sitting in this position that isn't a really life-altering position. So God comes into it even more so."[21]

Mike Huckabee, a two-time presidential candidate and former Southern Baptist pastor, insists he sees sincerity in Trump's proclamation of a prayerful life in a political world where sincerity and authenticity is on life support. Mindful of Trump's occasional bouts with crassness and moral missteps, Huckabee has said that Trump has a "deep, abiding respect, not just for God, but for all people who truly follow God. I think he's intrigued by it. I think it almost is something that he just finds amazing and fascinating. He has real respect for people of faith."[22]

Pope Francis, the worldwide leader of the Catholic Church, wasn't buying it. At the same time that Trump in 2016 was accusing fellow Republican presidential candidate Ted Cruz of telling lies (although without questioning Cruz's Christianity), Pope Francis was disputing Trump's profession of faith: "A person who thinks only about building walls, wherever they may be, and not building bridges, is not a Christian."

Trump's response:

> For a religious leader to question a person's faith is disgraceful. I am proud to be a Christian, and as President I will not allow Christianity to be consistently attacked and weakened, unlike what is happening now, with our current President (Barack Obama). No leader, especially a religious leader, should have the right to question another man's religion or faith."[23]

Long before he announced his candidacy for the presidency in 2015, Trump had already made connections with leaders in the Christian community such as Rev. Paula White, more than a decade earlier in fact. Within several years he was making more new friends in the world of evangelicalism, such as Ralph Reed, the first executive director of the Christian Coalition in the early 1990s and a longtime political consultant and lobbyist. With Reed, Trump shared conversations on topics such as the Christian faith worldview and values. Trump then met Huckabee through their frequent interactions at the Fox News studios in New York. And in November 2013, Donald and Melania attended the ninety-fifth birthday celebration for Billy Graham, which was an invitation-only event.

A major part of Trump's campaign agenda, and it remains so today, is to, in his words, "protect Christianity. And I can say that. I don't have to be politically correct." Trump caught the attention of evangelicals such as Reed by stating his belief that Christianity is under siege . . . and sticking to it. After Trump secured the Republican nomination for president in 2016, Reed took another look at where Trump stood on the issues most embraced by Christians and liked what he saw. His stamp of approval goes a long way in influencing evangelical leaders across America. "He was pro-life," Reed said of Trump. He went on to say,

> He had just released his list of twenty-one judges for the Supreme Court; he was pro-traditional marriage; he was pro-Israel; he was against the Iran nuclear deal; he was for defunding Planned Parenthood. He was solid on every key issue that we cared about. And Trump was the only candidate who made one of the central promises of his campaign—at least to social conservatives—the repealing of the Johnson Amendment [a provision added to the U.S. tax code in 1954 disallowing 501(c)(3) nonprofit entities from endorsing or opposing political candidates] and the restoring of First Amendment rights to churches and ministries.[24]

Some viewed this as Trump pandering to Reed and his evangelical teammates, but Reed shot down that idea. By then he had known Trump for more than six years and he shared with the New York billionaire what Reed described as "very heartfelt and transparent conversations that were not in the contest of a candidacy . . . I didn't flatter him. I gave him the best unvarnished understanding of my views."

Trump didn't just start seeking out Christian leaders and evangelicals right after announcing his candidacy in 2015; he had already established relationships with them, and in some cases had for more than a decade. To this day, he remains committed to his vast network of Christian contacts, often welcoming them into his closer circle time and again. Not all of them are Republicans, as is true with Bishop Wayne Jackson, a lifelong Democrat and the Detroit-based, African-American leader of Great Faith Ministries. When Jackson invited both Trump and Democrat nominee Hillary Clinton to speak to his congregation in 2016, Trump accepted immediately; Clinton turned it down. On the day Trump showed up to speak, a bevy of protestors greeted his arrival outside, but "when he got out of the SUV, the Spirit of the Lord told me that's the next president of the United States," Jackson said of Trump.[25]

One of the speakers at the 2016 Republican National Convention was Darrell Scott, an African-American pastor from Cleveland and devoted Trump supporter, even amid rising racial tensions across America following the shooting of five Dallas policemen by a gunman who had been on the prowl for white people. While much of the media chose to stir up charges of racism against Trump, Scott, accompanied by his wife Belinda, boldly went to the convention in support of Trump, not only as a political figure but also for his being a brother in Christ. The Scotts knew Trump well by then; they had already been acquainted with him for five years, since 2011.

"He really is pursuing a deeper spiritual life. I can sense it," Belinda Scott said. "My prayer for Mr. Trump is that he will be more sensitive to God than he ever has before . . . something is going on." Added Darrell Scott: "He's the first one to admit, 'I'm flawed. I'm not perfect. I need to do better. I need to be better.'"[26]

Trump's associations with men and women in Christian ministry are many. They have been years in the making in many cases, and they are evidence of his own walk with God and a strong faith that is as much about the company you keep as what you say and do. Others who know him well and will attest to his sincerity of faith include Dallas evangelist Lance Wallnau, who claims he heard from the Lord that the forty-fifth president would be an Isaiah 45 president, which he interpreted to mean Donald Trump. Wallnau said that Trump would be a leader much in the spirit of Cyrus depicted in Isaiah 45 of the Old Testament—a leader appointed by God.[27] While not openly endorsing Trump for president, Franklin Graham, Billy Graham's evangelistic son, nonetheless said in an interview with the Religion News Service, "I think maybe God has allowed Donald Trump to win this election to protect the nation for the next few years by giving maybe an opportunity to have some good judges."[28]

In the 2016 election, Trump won a decisive Electoral College victory despite Hillary Clinton winning the popular vote by a margin of 2.9 million votes. Many Christians saw this as a sign of God's Providence. His presidency has done more to advance the Christian Right cause than just protect the makeup of federal courts. One of the hallmarks of his presidency has been the White House access he has afforded evangelicals, signaling his commitment to move pro-life efforts forward in spite of an uphill battle. Further, his executive order took the teeth out of the Johnson Amendment. Trump's official direction to the Department of the Treasury was to not take "any adverse action against" clergy members, churches, or other faith-based organizations "on the basis that such individual organization speaks or has spoken about moral or political issues from a religious perspective." At the time of the executive order, though, it was still left to Congress to complete the process by repealing the Johnson Amendment, and with a Democratic-controlled House of Representatives as of 2020, that prospect appeared unlikely.[29]

Election Day 2016 dawned with many Trump supporters seriously concerned about late polls showing Clinton several percentage points ahead of Trump. His election was in doubt. Even Trump, ever confident about his chances of victory (at least publicly), wasn't sure what to expect. "I don't know, Jerry, these exit polls look bad," Trump reportedly said in an Election Night phone call with Jerry Falwell, Jr., president of Liberty University, an evangelical liberal arts institution in Lynchburg, Virginia. Trump had spoken there earlier in the year, showcasing his Christian beliefs with enthusiasm, and now he needed some support in return from Falwell.

"No, no, no, you got it," Falwell told Trump. "I just have a feeling. You're going to win it. I know it. Too much has happened that's been miraculous this year for it not to be of God. You're going to win." Once it became clear several hours later, with one key battleground state after another turning to Trump, that he was headed to victory, Trump again spoke to Falwell, with buoyancy, saying, "Jerry, we're about to win. They're about to announce that we're going to win Pennsylvania."

"That's the game," Falwell responded.

"Yup, that'll be the game," Trump said.[30]

A year later, after being inaugurated in January 2017, Trump returned to Liberty University to give a graduation address to more than fifty thousand in attendance. It was a captive, faith-based audience, of course, that enthusiastically welcomed Trump "home". He stated:

> It's been a little over a year since I've spoken on your beautiful campus and so much has changed. Right here, the class of 2017, dressed in cap and gown, graduating to a totally brilliant future. And here I am standing before you as president of the United States. So I'm guessing there are some people here today who thought that either one of those things, either one, would really require major help from God. Do we agree? And we got it.[31]

Chapter Three

Prizefighter

"The probability that we may fall in the struggle ought not to deter us from the support of a cause we believe to be just; it shall not deter me . . . standing up boldly and alone and hurling defiance . . ."

-Lincoln's Speech, Springfield, Ill. House of Representatives, Dec. 26, 1839

YOU DON'T WIN A FOUR-YEAR, ALL-EXPENSES-PAID STAY AT THE LUXURIous White House by going at life (and political opponents) wearing white gloves. Campaigning for the office of the U.S. presidency can be a dirt-thrown slog through a gauntlet of assorted "enemy" troops, among them stop-at-nothing political opponents and a press eager to take you down.

Requirements for such a calling include nerves of titanium, the hide of a Little League umpire made thick by parental dissent, the oratorical skills of a Winston Churchill, the courage of a stand-up comedian performing before a packed house of strangers, the resiliency of a Navy SEAL wannabe in training, and the cunning and pugilistic skills of a Muhammad Ali.

Donald Trump fights the good fight; in his own personally modified ways, he does it better than any of his rivals. A hound dog media and an increasingly corrupt deep state are hard at work trying to foil his every move while at the same time he remains relevant in the ongoing fight of a bitterly divisive nation.

Donald Trump craves a good fight. He's never shy about mixing it up with political, media, or business opponents. He doesn't need a barroom (he doesn't even drink), but he savors a good brawl, and battleground states are his forte. Just tell him it's impossible and he already has a plan to get it done. During a 2020 presidential campaign appearance at a Fox News town hall in Scranton, Pennsylvania in March 2020, Trump mentioned the media when asked by an audience member about his controversial rhetoric. He responded with fighting words.

I wouldn't be sitting here (as president) if I had turned the other cheek," Trump added. "When they hit us, we have to hit back; I feel that. We get hit so hard, and we have a media that I'd say, to a large extent, is part of the Democrat Party, it really is. It's terrible. It's unfair. I call it 'fake news' and people are using that all over the world now. That's the way it is . . . If we don't fight back, you won't be a fan of mine for very long.[1]

Those who knew Trump when he was a kid might have seen this coming. He was a young boy, a second grader, sometimes known as "Donnie," when he threw a punch at a music teacher, giving the man a black eye. "I punched my music teacher because I didn't think he knew anything about music, and I almost got expelled," Trump later bragged.[2]

The fight goes on decades later. Welcome to Donald Trump's world. "He's a complicated man who is not prone to introspection, nostalgia, or patience," news commentator Bill O'Reilly wrote in his 2019 book.[3]

Trump's competitive persona had begun with his fascination with brick and mortar. From an early age, he would tag along with his father to construction sites, where Trump the elder was both boss and handyman, getting down and dirty with his men working construction, demonstrating a 1950s version of servant-leadership. Of the five Trump children, Donnie was the only one to show a strong interest in following in his father's footsteps in the construction business. It fueled his competitive fires from an early age with the desire to build things bigger and better than anyone else.

One of Donald's favorite stories that he sometimes shares with others recounts one day when he was eight years old—around the same time he was making his music teacher a knuckle sandwich—he grabbed his younger brother Robert's toy blocks and constructed a giant skyscraper out of them, gluing them together and never returning them. This was Donnie's way of constructing a fantasy that would guide his life for the next fifty-plus years—ultimately changing Manhattan's skyline in the process.[4]

Six years after the elementary school episode, Fred Trump moved his thirteen-year-old son out of school and enrolled him at New York Military Academy in Cornwall, New York, an institution founded in 1889 and situated about fifty miles north of the city. What finally pushed Fred to send his son upstate was that Donald, by then a young teen, would sneak away from the family's middle-class Jamaica home in Queens to accompany buddies to a guys' day out in the Times Square area of Manhattan. Somewhere along the way, Donald got his hands on switchblade knives he brought home. Eventually his Mom and Dad discovered the knives. Fred expected better from his five children, but his long hours working at his job sites kept him away from home much of the time, hindering his ability to properly discipline the energetic and sometimes unruly and obstinate Donnie. Fred felt he needed to provide discipline via surrogate. So, military school it was.

Young Donald was in eighth grade at the time, and his dad believed the change to a more disciplined environment would do his son good. It did, putting young Trump in a structured, albeit harsh setting where he could channel his aggression into achievement and eventually graduate in 1964 with the rank of cadet captain. A National Public Radio (NPR) report republished by O'Reilly in *The United States of Trump* sheds more light on the strict experience:

> Back in Trump's day, cadets would wake up near the crack of dawn, hurry into uniforms, and march in formation to breakfast. First-year cadets had to eat their meals squared-off—lifting their forks in a right angle into their mouths. And after breakfast they'd scurry back to clean their rooms for inspection.[5]

Fighting the good fight, but on his own terms, is what drives Donald Trump. To borrow a pet phrase from O'Reilly—one of the few in the media to make a friendly connection to Trump—"bold and fresh" is an accurate depiction of Trump. In his own words, he might say, "I did, and do, things my way." During precious free time away from the rigors of academic studies and military drills at the military academy, Trump loved to hang out in his dorm room and "hit the beach." He would insert an ultraviolet light bulb into the ceiling light fixture, then lie down on his bunk and kick back, pretending he was soaking up Florida sunshine. Author Gwenda Blair writes,

> Dropping the usual Trump family reticence about their wealth, (Trump) pegged his father's worth at $30 million and bragged that the number doubled every year. "Donald had a sense of how he wanted to be viewed," (senior-year roommate David Smith) said. "He really wanted to be a success. He was already focused on the future, thinking long-term more than present. He used to talk about his dad's business, how he would use him as a role model but go one step further."[6]

Fred Trump was a mentor as much as a father figure to Donald, and Donald himself was an eager—how else can you say it?—apprentice. There wasn't noticeable tension or contention between the two, but it was evident that Donald was not reluctant about standing up to his old man. By his late teens, Donald refusing to be intimidated by Fred. All the while, he was cultivating skills that would serve him well in the business world, the world of reality-TV entertainment (*The Apprentice*, which ran eleven seasons on NBC) and, finally, the cutthroat, life-on-the-edge world of politics—presidential politics. Note that Trump was the first person ever elected U.S. president without having previously served in elective office or the military.

Michael D'Antonio, author of *Never Enough*, described Donald Trump's relationship with his dad in saying,

> Learning from what he saw, Donald resolved to stand up to anyone who challenged him, including his father. Years later, he would say, 'I used to fight back all the time. My father was one tough son of a gun.' However, he added, 'My father respects me because I stood up to him.'[7]

It wasn't just Manhattan skyscrapers that rocket-fueled Trump's imagination, pumped helium into his oversized ego, and positioned him in full fight mode. Bigger and better could manifest itself in other ways in a manner keeping with what he did best—develop real estate. He wanted to be famous. We know how that worked out—literally, stamped in twenty-foot letters on more than one big city skyscraper.

Trump undertook his first major construction project, on his own and out from under Fred Sr.'s wings, in his mid-twenties. It started out in his head as ostentatious plans for a 30,000-unit apartment complex, spread over two properties in Manhattan. If successfully completed, it would be the world's largest such apartment project, containing more units than all of the projects his father's Trump Organization had built over the years.[8] It would be one confident boy/man's hubris executed to the nth degree.

Trump had procured an option on the old Penn Central rail yards, and that's where he would build. Before breaking ground, though, he needed the properties to be rezoned from industrial to residential—encompassing two sites; one at 60th Street and the other at 34th Street. He also needed to persuade banks to help finance the massive construction. Before he could plow his way through either of those obstacles, though, he would need to come up with a design for the complex project conforming to codes. At times it seemed he would've had better luck building an escalator worthy of replacing Jack's beanstalk. A lot to ask for.

Trump's pie-in-the-sky plan called for 20,000 units to be built at the 60th Street yards and another 10,000 at 34th Street, with no railroads running beneath them. There were other hurdles to negotiate as well. First, the only way to pay for basic (yet exorbitant) infrastructure items such as streets, sewers, and waterlines would be to build thousands more units than community residents and leaders would be amenable to. Second, without community support, the odds of getting the zoning change were essentially nil. Undeterred, Trump hired one of the city's most prestigious architectural firms to design the companion complexes, even with financing issues threatening to put a halt to his plans. There wasn't much money available to invest in such a gargantuan endeavor, especially one conceived by a relative neophyte, new to how the game was played in Manhattan. In terms of construction costs, the city and the State of New York were close to broke. Plus, federal housing subsidies that had once been the financial lifeblood for Fred Trump's ventures a generation earlier had dried up due to cutbacks from the Nixon administration.[9]

Trump with his entourage of architects, attorneys, and consultants—a publicity manager, too—stayed in formation and continued to march through a phalanx of countless meetings, phone calls, letters, naysayers, and communities in opposition. But there was only so much they could do. Gradually, Trump had to scale down his construction plans in order to keep cracking open doors. His architects' renderings got down to 5,000 units—significantly less than the original 30,000, yet that was still too many for local community approval, and the meetings between Trump and the community board grew more antagonistic.

At times, Fred Trump would attend the community meetings, sitting in the back of the auditorium while watching his son give a buoyant presentation complete with colorful slides of parks and trees fronting shadowy groups of yet-to-be-built buildings. Donald's presentation skills became more polished with each occurrence.[10]

Still, Trump's fresh tactics were going nowhere. He needed a viable Plan B for the development of the rail yards to get some sort of return on his investment. Almost magically, Plan B materialized in the form of the city's desire to build a new convention center to replace a 1950s-constructed facility that now, in the 1970s, was obsolete. City planners, with Mayor Abe Beame's approval, had chosen a 44th Street site near Times Square. The city's blueprint showed a modern convention center with a projected $231 million price tag, featuring a bold, futuristic design. Once completed, the space-age facility would be supported by a spaceport platform, extending out hundreds of feet over the Hudson River.

Recognizing opportunity, and making use of new connections he had made chasing his 30,000-unit dream, Trump made the paradigm shift. His new dream: a convention center, built on a significantly reduced budget. He knew the 34th Street rail yards would easily accommodate his team's own design. No longer would there be a need for annoying zoning alterations. This was adaptability at work. Now Donald had a fight he could win. His design associates told him they could design and build a magnificent two-story, bronze-colored-glass structure at about half the cost of the city's 44th Street plan. It would all be on land, and it would feature ample space for trucks to load and unload without causing traffic snarls.[11]

Listening closely to his adviser's input, Trump devised a bold marketing and publicity plan for what he called "The Miracle on 34th Street," in honor of the classic Christmas movie. Soon he was giving pitches and presentations to private audiences of influential community leaders. At one point, however, Beame threw a monkey wrench into Trump's construction plans, switching his support from the 44th Street site now being labeled untenable to an alternate site at Battery Park City. Trump stubbornly pushed ahead on his 34th Street proposal, keenly and aggressively drumming up public support to elevate his conception above Beame's. He got word out through the media that Battery Park City (BPC) was a bad choice, one of his newsworthy press releases calling BPC a "rip-off." Further support came from a prominent labor negotiator, who told *The New York Times* that a convention center built in Battery Park City would be like "putting a nightclub in a graveyard."[12]

Trump won the fight! He got his convention center at 34th Street, creating thousands of jobs in the process. Blair put it this way:

> The real 'Miracle on 34th Street' was not the actual convention center design that was unveiled that day. It was how Donald Trump had managed to combine his father's political connections, his advisers' collective wisdom, and his own budding development acumen to outmaneuver his competitors.[13]

Trump is far from being an undefeated champion in the ring of business, media, and politics, but many of his other skirmishes are worth mentioning.

In the wake of his 34th Street "Miracle", Trump jumped at the chance to pull off another major real-estate development coup. This one involved the once preeminent Commodore hotel, boasting two thousand guest rooms, built in 1919 next to New York City's perpetually busy Grand Terminal. This city landmark was named after legendary railroad magnate Commodore Vanderbilt. For Trump, this job wasn't going to be the construction of something new and shiny from the ground up; this time it would be restoration of a hotel once teeming with affluent visitors but now falling apart at the seams from the inside out. Entire floors had been roped off as unusable. Hookers propositioned clients in the lobby, and ownership was in arrears of $6.6 million in real-estate taxes on a hotel losing $1 million a year. Trump acknowledged the unseemly grunginess, but he also saw great opportunity. This time the obstacles included an estimated purchase price of $10 million, a desperate need for a city-authorized tax abatement, and a remodeling proposition possibly requiring a gutting of the building. Just for starters.[14]

Again, Trump went to work on multiple levels, whacking his way through miles of red tape and minions of doubting Thomases. He called on and met with architects, city officials, bankers. He even met with a member of the renowned Chicago-based Pritzker family, owners of the Hyatt chain of upscale hotels. At the time, none of their hotels were based in New York City, so Trump tried to (and succeeded at) convincing them to buy in to his plans. It was a slew of insurmountable tasks, and it took many months of showing off and touting impressive-looking and sounding plans, cajoling, and arranging ever more meetings. Trump ultimately bullied and cajoled his way through the dustup storms and smoke-filled meeting rooms and restaurants to pull together all the disparate pieces to make it happen. He had rescued the Commodore from either a wrecking ball or oblivion in restoring it and repopulating it—much to the delight of his accountants. In the process, he impressed power brokers from one city borough to the next. Fred's kid had his stuff together.

Fast forward to the mid-1980s, where we find Trump, about to turn forty, in a verbal war with New York City Mayor Ed Koch. For the first time, it's business mixed with real politics as The Donald comes out swinging, blasting city government for its lackluster performance at renovating

Wollman Rink in Central Park. This popular venue was designed to allow skaters to bask in their daily reenactments of Currier & Ives-like scenery, especially around Christmastime.

The rink's renovations, which had begun in 1980, were still dragging on into 1986. It was a classic example of governmental agencies not getting the job done, and Trump took notice. This time his punching bag was the embattled Koch, and the verbal war played out in the city's media. The argument—and the inefficiency of the renovations—quickly ended when Trump agreed to finish the job himself, at no expense to the city. He completed the rink's fixes in three months at a cost to himself that was well below what the city had budgeted. Trump claimed victory, revealed more wasteful spending of taxpayer dollars, and gained the kudos of many in the city.[15]

Note that in his best-selling 1987 book *The Art of the Deal* (fifty-two weeks on best-seller lists, including *The New York Times*), Trump opens by saying, "I don't do it for the money." That might be laughable to his critics and even many of his supporters, but it has a ring of sincerity to David Brody and Scott Lamb. They write,

> Though we have avoided playing the part of an armchair psychologist with Donald Trump, several people we interviewed who consider themselves to be friends or on friendly terms with Trump stated their opinion that they don't believe Donald Trump's relationship with money flows from a heart of greed... These off-the-record friendly interviewees sense that Trump's ambition stems from a deep-rooted need to command respect—a basic, simple drive to prove that he is the best.[16]

Trump not only relished such tussles, he feasted on them. Longtime business associate Ned Eichler said this about his occasional golfing rival: "The biggest project, the one with the most apartments, that's what was exciting to him. He thrived on conflict, the bigger the better. He loved it. People like him always do."[17]

Eighteen Republican candidates filed to run for president in the 2016 election, and Donald Trump's entry into the contest was greeted by the usual cavalcade of guffaws and insults from Democrats and many in the media. But by the time of the 2016 Republican National Convention in Cleveland ended on July 21, Trump was the last candidate standing. Written off by most pundits at the beginning, Trump steadily rose through the ranks of GOP candidates to ultimately take down Texas Senator Ted Cruz, whom he vanquished by a final delegate count of more than three to one.

Along the way, Trump broke many of the unwritten rules of campaign and debate performance, generating record crowds at his rallies and turning televised debates into must-see TV. He also did some poking and bomb lobbing of his own, ridiculing Florida Senator Marco Rubio for being vertically challenged ("Little Marco," the 6-foot-3 Trump kept calling him) and former Hewlett Packard CEO Carly Fiorina for her physical appearance ("Look at the face! Would anyone vote for that?" Trump remarked to a *Rolling Stone* magazine reporter when Fiorina's face popped up on a nearby TV screen). Just when you thought Trump's unpresidential posturing would mean a loss of support, his numbers kept going up.

At one point the debate turned into a war with sexist overtones between Trump and Fox News moderator Megyn Kelly. This was after Kelly had posed a question for Trump that he—and many pundits watching— thought was more accusatory than inquisitive, as Bill O'Reilly would later describe in his book. The next day, Trump, speaking on CNN, took a swipe at Kelly, facetiously saying of her, "You could see she had blood coming out of her eyes, blood coming out of . . . wherever." The reaction across America was swift and condemning. Trump later said he had meant to say "nose" in place of "wherever," the latter an apparent reference to a woman's menstrual cycle.[18] Trump was financing most of his campaign, so he wasn't worried about losing donors. When updated polls came out, he was still well ahead in the Republican field. He was, in a sense, politically bulletproof, and when he went through with his pledge to skip the next Fox News-sponsored debate unless the network removed Kelly as one of the moderators, there was no stopping him, at least in the GOP world.

O'Reilly wrote:

> That was a turning point for candidate Trump. He began to understand that his in-your-face presentation was actually inoculating him against bad press and pressure groups. The more outrageous his rhetoric, the firmer his supporters stood by him. Modern politics had never seen anything like this.[19]

Marco Rubio tried these same ultra-honest, slap-in-the-face tactics, which fell flat. Apparently, only Donald Trump could act like Donald Trump and get away with it.

Once Trump was elected president in November 2016, the hits kept coming. Opponents would take a roundhouse swing and miss, and Trump would bob and weave before throwing a haymaker at his latest opponent's kisser. Here are a few highlights:

When some National Football League players started taking the lead of activist San Francisco 49ers quarterback Colin Kaepernick in kneeling in protest during the pre-game playing of the national anthem, Trump shot down the players' actions, saying, "You have to stand proudly for the national anthem, or you shouldn't be playing, you shouldn't be there. Maybe you shouldn't be in the country," Trump said, having at one time referred to the activist players as "SOBs" during a speech in Alabama.[20]

When Special Counsel Robert Mueller ended his twenty-two-month investigation into alleged collusion ties between Russia and Trump regarding the 2016 election, Mueller's conclusion being that there was insufficient evidence to charge Trump with a crime, Trump simply said, "The case is closed! Thank you."[21]

When House Speaker Nancy Pelosi spearheaded impeachment hearings in 2019 against Trump over the content of a telephone conversation between him and Ukrainian president Volodymyr Zelensky in July 2019, Trump simply referred to his accusers as the "do-nothing Democrats," while he was leaving the country to fly to London to attend a NATO summit, tweeting, "Heading to Europe to represent our Country and fight hard for the American People while the Do Nothing Democrats purposely scheduled an Impeachment Hoax hearing on the same date as NATO. Not nice!"[22] While House Democrats had a healthy majority to rubber stamp articles of impeachment sent forward to the Senate, Republicans had the upper hand in the Senate, where it would take 67 votes to oust Trump. Arguments were made on both sides in a Senate trial presided over by Supreme Court Chief Justice John Roberts. Acting as jurors, senators voted to acquit Trump by a count of 52-48. Again, Trump had fought and survived, even though the odds against his being found guilty in a fervently partisan Senate had been stacked higher than Trump Tower.

When Donald Trump in 2021 went from President back to candidate all over again, amidst ongoing indictments, lawfare, trumped-up charges, and trials presided over by politically motivated partisans meant to eliminate him from the 2024 Presidential race, he staged a political comeback unprecedented in American history. Trump won the 2024 Iowa Caucuses with record numbers, doubling his support from the 2016 Iowa contest.[23]

He became on of only two Republican candidates ever to win the New Hampshire primary three times (Richard Nixon did it first).[24] And on he went, in bare-knuckle, full-fight mode against any and all challengers. He assured the nation once again he was the unmistakable leader of the Republican Party. The increasing support from political leaders as well as voters despite arrests and show trials revealed one thing—millions of Americans were not ready to step out of the ring, yet . . . and neither was he.

Trump pulls no punches and maneuvers like a Mike Tyson heavyweight, opting for the in-your-face offense to dancing around opponents. Donald Trump has spent his life fighting. In his book *Time To Get Tough*–published in 2011, four years before he tossed his hat into the presidential ring–Trump revealed his simple philosophy: "I always believe when attacked, hit your opponent back harder and meaner and ideally right between the eyes." [25]

Chapter Four

Uncommonly Common

"Common looking people are the best in the world; that is the reason the Lord makes so many of them."

-Lincoln recounting a remark in a dream to his
secretary John Hay, Dec. 23, 1863

HALF OF AMERICA WILL FIND THIS DIFFICULT TO SWALLOW, BUT DONALD Trump is a regular guy—as regular as a billionaire U.S. president can be. He is a working-class kind of guy who resonates with blue-collar types, even those who haven't met him. Shortly after Trump won the 2016 presidential election, CNN interviewed such a person—a working-class guy, much like the hordes who turn out by the millions to vote for him—to get his take on Trump's upset victory. No doubt the man made CNN staffers squirm when he said that Trump reminded him of his own father, a family man with an ironclad work ethic. His dad had worked at blue-collar jobs most of his life, the man told CNN, only for his way of life to get scrapped because of politicians and technocrats out for themselves at the expense of the underclass.

"I don't know if Trump will change anything," the grown-up son said, fighting his emotions, "and I don't really care if he does. He is the only one who spoke to my dad's broken heart. My dad is now gone, but when I voted for Trump, it was like voting for my dad."[1]

Donald Trump is no ordinary Joe (far from it) but he is a man of the people—and he won't debate or fight back against anyone who describes him as a "populist"—a label that doesn't often get attached to too many billionaires. He is not a man of pretension and is not reticent to let down his guard in public, with or without a microphone in front of him.

One of many stories reflecting Trump's ordinary-man character describes a time during his 2016 presidential campaign Trump was finished giving a speech at a small venue somewhere out in America. Following his talk and after leaving the stage, as described by Gene Ho in his book

Trump by, Trump walked the halls of the building to retreat to the "green m," offering a sanctuary away from the crowd. "It was a comfortable room, one with retractable walls to adjust to a suitable size. The room was mostly bare, nothing too fancy, but the tables were draped in cloth and refreshments were available," writes Ho, who at the time was a photographer tethered to Trump during the campaign.[2]

Just as the door to the room was closed behind him, Trump breathed a noticeable sigh of relief. He picked up a bottle of water, removed the top, and poured some of the water on his hands, which he rubbed together to clean them off. He leaned forward a bit, and using his still-wet hands, wiped away the sweat on his face. He then grabbed the loose end of a tablecloth and dried his face with it. This was not the act of a man on guard, afraid to refresh himself in a manner that any ordinary person probably would have done in like circumstances. Miss Manners would not have approved, but thumbs up from Bob the Truck Driver.

"I stood in awe," Ho wrote. "The man who I had seen as a seemingly indestructible force for months appeared so raw and human in that moment... In this unedited act, I was reminded immediately who stood before me: a man. He is just a man. He sweats, he bleeds, and he's flawed."[3]

Trump brings to mind Howard Cosell, the renowned Brooklyn-raised sports announcer and commentator whose calling card during his 40 years behind the mic was "telling it like it is." Cosell was an ego-driven media icon for whom there was no in-between, his fame largely built on his fourteen seasons as part of ABC-TV's vaunted Monday Night Football coverage. When sports fans were polled on their favorite sports announcers, Cosell was voted Favorite and Least Favorite—at the same time. Applied to the world of 21st century politics, that's Trump—embraced and detested simultaneously.

Trump tells—and tweets—it like it is, much in Cosell mode. He's all about straight talk, simple language (using few words with more than two syllables), and shooting straight without a filter. He says what he means, and means what he says. Anybody can understand what he's saying—as annoying as the message might be for liberal elitists insulted by such brash language. His supporters listen to him and think, *that's exactly what I was thinking.* Trump knows his audience, and it begins with not speaking down to them but in concert with them. That's how he's made a strong connection with tens of millions of people. He doesn't speak above his audiences, instead choosing to meet them at their level. Whatever his arrogance factor might be on a given day, it doesn't hurt his ability to communicate with the masses and be easily understood. "I manage to blast through the ridiculous liberal bias of the media and speak right to the hearts of the people—or at least I try," Trump has said. "Even New York magazine, hardly a conservative outlet, has given me credit for shaking up the status quo." [4]

Before Trump became president, he was perhaps best known for his starring role in the hit TV reality series *The Apprentice*, which aired for fifteen seasons between 2004 and 2017. Like anything else Trump has been involved in, the show had its enthusiastic followers as well as its detractors, but it did elevate Trump to iconic status in America—and in other parts of the world—mostly because of his brashness as well as his conciseness. When it was time for a contestant to leave the show, Trump simply said "You're fired!" and that person was gone. That's telling it like it is.

"Those of you who have watched *The Apprentice* will notice that the candidates who can present the facts with the least amount of verbal decoration will have an advantage," Trump wrote in his 2010 book *Think Like a Champion*.

> We don't have the time for loquacious colleagues, and the long winded diatribes we often have to suffer through will greatly diminish their chances of winning.

> Simple as it sounds, there is great wisdom in the short, fast, and direct route. Knowing where you're going in your conversation and demonstrating to others you know where you're going by being concise, is a big step toward leadership and respect . . . People appreciate brevity in today's world. [5]

Often brief, blunt, and confrontational, Trump is also intolerant of contrarians—many disguised as journalists—who emerge from the woodwork to challenge any of his positions or statements that don't fit the politically correct narrative. Trump came to the White House as an outsider, a businessman without a political pedigree. On one hand he fulfilled the wishes of voters who had long awaited such a paradigm shift in Washington, D.C.; on the other hand, his election peeved capitol insiders—many of them manning media outposts—who refused to tolerate anything but politics as usual.

One aspect of Trump's character that gets lost in the media dust storm that engulfs him is his capacity for compassion. In *Think Like a Champion*,

Trump recalls the time in 1988 when he received a desperate plea from a Los Angeles rabbi—someone he had never met—asking the New York businessman for help in getting his three-year-old son to New York City in hopes that doctors there could find a cure for the boy's severe respiratory condition. The request was a considerable one: would Trump fly the boy to New York City in his private jet. No commercial airline would allow the boy to fly on one of their flights because of the extensive medical equipment he needed to have with him at all times.

"I had small children at the time, and I immediately said yes to his request. How could I say no?" Trump writes. The future president sent his private jet to Los Angeles to pick up the boy and his parents and bring them to New York City. Although the meeting with health-care experts proved futile as the young boy soon died, the boy's parents never forgot Trump's generosity. In *Think Like a Champion*, Trump reported that the dad had contacted him every year for eighteen years running, doing so on the day before the Jewish holiday Rosh Hashanah, to convey a message of thanks while telling Trump of the blessings they'd had in their lives. [6]

Numerous other instances of Trump's Samaritan ways date back decades before he entered politics. In 1991, his mother, Mary Anne Trump, then seventy-nine years old was assaulted and robbed in Queens—knocked to the ground by a teenager who made off with what cash she had on her. Her fall to the ground broke her ribs, induced hemorrhaging in her brain and resulted in a permanent disability involving her vision and hearing. A witness to the incident, a truck driver, chased down and apprehended the sixteen-year-old boy. It turned out the truck driver hero's home was about to be foreclosed, and Trump graciously wrote him a check that allowed the man to pay his mortgage. [7] Evangelist James Robison said,

> I've been back behind the curtain with him when he's with people nobody sees, and he keeps noticing the crippled person... or the military person, or the person with the police force, or the person that looks like they're poor. Those are the people he goes to when nobody sees him. He notices them. He notices them when he walks out in the crowd. He'll notice the people that nobody else notices. [8]

Empathy and compassion are a core part of Trump's makeup—the part that most of the media never reports. He is at his best in that regard when he is out of the public eye, as was the case in August 2016 when prolonged rains in southern Louisiana produced floods that drove many families from their homes, devastating the area. Tens of thousands of homes and many businesses were submerged, with overall damage to the area estimated at between $10 billion and $15 billion. One of those homeowners affected was Tony Perkins, a campaign supporter of Trump's and, at the time, an interim pastor at a large church.

Four days passed, and still there was no governmental assistance. No President Barack Obama onsite to see the damage and console residents. No Hillary Clinton, then the Democratic presidential nominee, either. Seemingly no presidential-level interest, until Trump showed up accompanied by his vice-presidential candidate Mike Pence and evangelist Franklin Graham, son of Billy.

"Trump was visibly taken aback by how significant the devastation and destruction was," Perkins said. "He told the Secret Service to stop the cars, and he got out and went up and met residents in the neighborhoods. He was so warm and genuine in his concern."

One of the then-homeless Louisiana couples Trump met was Jimmy and Olive Morgan, who, when asked by Trump if they were going to rebuild, said they were "getting up there" in years and didn't know if they had it in them to build another home. At which point, according to Pence, Trump reached over and grabbed Jimmy Morgan by the shoulder and said, "You're going to rebuild; I know you're that kind of guy. You're going to rebuild." Nine months later, Pence returned to check in on the couple, and found out that they had indeed rebuilt their home. [9]

Donald Trump has been described as "a wrecking ball to the spirit of political correctness."[10] It fits, and it's a description Trump himself would probably agree with and consider a badge of honor. He says what he thinks, so much of which enters airspace as unfiltered sound waves. Along with that, he also produces moments of self-deprecating humor that progressive media often just don't seem to grasp. When he poked fun at the notion that he might somehow try to wrangle a third four-year term as president (the U.S. Constitution limits a president to two elected terms), many of his political opponents and even some in the media expressed sincere disdain. Ditto in August 2018 when, at a veterans' event in Louisville, Kentucky, Trump was obviously joking when he wanted to award himself the Medal of Honor, saying "I wanted one, but they (his aides) told me I don't qualify. I said, 'Can I give it to myself anyway?' They said, 'I don't think that's a good idea.'"[11] Again, his comments were taken seriously by many lacking the humor gene.

Here's what Trump is up against. U.S. presidents are generally expected to speak and act with a certain sense of decorum that supposedly suits the office—a well-bred concoction with ingredients that include humility, poise, gravitas, temperance, empathy, and dignity. The common man (or woman) might possess one or two of those qualities on a good day, but the American president is often considered ill-suited for office if he or she is lacking in any of those areas. Aside from his billions, Donald Trump is more common man than he is refined national leader. Again, Trump probably wouldn't argue with that because he doesn't care. He is not part of the enlightened elites that many political enemies embrace. He can be downright uncouth, graceless, and even odd.

Self-restraint is not a Trump strong point. In his book *Trump's America*, Newt Gingrich mentions "Trump's ferocity in counter-attacking (as) part of his strategy." Gingrich continues:

As someone who spent his career with blue-collar workers, Trump understands that someone punching you becomes an existential moment. You either fight back or you back down. Trump always chooses to fight. In some ways, President Trump is the first president since Andrew Jackson to understand barroom brawling at a practical level. He applies this brawl model to politics. You have to counterpunch or you will lose.[12]

In his book *Understanding Trump*, published a year before his *Trump's America*, Gingrich says that to understand Trump, you have to delve into his psychology as well as his philosophy:

"To really grasp Trump, you must understand his doctrine and his psychology—the collection of attitudes and methods he uses to achieve success. That doctrine is fast, aggressive, disruptive, and confounding to the unwary . . . He places a greater emphasis on speed than mistake avoidance, sets big goals and remains flexible. He capitalizes on his opponents' weaknesses and works relentlessly to diminish or avoid their strengths."[13]

Once Trump thinks it, he speaks it. Why is that so hard to understand? Run-on sentences are the bane of Trump's speaking style. Sometimes he'll speak it before he has finished processing the thought. But this is a manner of communication that endears him to the common man and woman. That is how they speak themselves, whether gathered around the dinner table or cozying up to the local bar. It is a healthy mix of shooting from the hip and exercising a sense of humor that begs a thick skin. If you're not comfortable talking straight and find Trump distasteful, then you are probably spending much of your life with a frown on your face.

Then there are the Trump tweets. Among the untold thousands:

"It used to be cars were made in Flint and you couldn't drink the water in Mexico. Now cars are made in Mexico and you can't drink the water in Flint."

"I have this thing called Twitter and Facebook, which is amazing actually. It's like owning The New York Times without the losses."

"My biggest opponent was the microphone." (After one of his 2016 debates against Hillary Clinton)

"The sheer volume of people that support him because he's willing to be funny and ballsy and say what he thinks—you cannot underestimate that," an unnamed senior Trump administration official was quoted as saying by politico.com in October 2018. Added Brian O. Walsh, president of the pro-Trump group America First Action, "His speaking style is what endears him to his supporters. It's a big part of what fueled him through the (2016) primaries and the general election. The unpolished everyman who says what he thinks."[14]

For years, the most obvious target of ridicule from the anti-Trumpers has been Trump's hair. Is it his or a toupee? Occasionally Trump has played along, such as in those times he has invited people up on stage with him to let them take a good tug. It doesn't come off. It isn't a hairpiece. Audiences love it when he puts out such a challenge, and the hair stays in place.

"Another time he had us laughing until it hurt," author Gene Ho says in *Trumpography*. "He delivered a stand-up-worthy string of one-liners about how he'd contemplated the effects of global warming because he preferred aerosol hairspray to pump action. Then he went on to mimic the chht, chht, chht sound of the individual pumps from the squirt bottle. 'We're going to be here all day with pump-action hairspray!'"[15]

"It pays to have a sense of humor about yourself," Trump said, recalling a credit-card commercial he once made, in which a gust of wind atop Trump Tower blew the card out of Trump's hand, sending it down to the street below, the scene ending with Trump climbing out of a dumpster after retrieving his card while a passerby remarked, "And I thought he was doing so well!" Trump said. "If I took myself too seriously, I would have missed out on a lot of fun and a nice paycheck."[16]

Like any normal person, Trump experienced some episodes he would rather were forgotten. Like the time in an archived Saturday Night Live skit from 2004, Trump dodged the feathered bird costume to settle on a yellow suit instead. It was a comic scene later used by social media to ridicule him. Thankfully, he nixed the feathers ahead of time.

Donald Trump sports a physical persona unmistakable in a crowd, and a personality beyond unique. As Candidate Trump or as President Trump, he is loved and hated simultaneously—especially hated by his political opponents and by the press and media of the day. Yet he continues to command the respect and endearment of ordinary folk. It doesn't take good looks, or a genius IQ. All it takes is that common connection. That's all.

Chapter Five
All in the Family

"So this is the little lady that all us folks in Washington like so much. Don't you ever come 'round here asking me to do some of those impossible things you women always ask for, for I would have to do it, and then I'd get into trouble."

-Abraham Lincoln to the actress Rose Eytinge (no date)

DONALD TRUMP ENTERED THE WHITE HOUSE WITH FIRST LADY MELANIA (his third wife after two failed marriages) with his fifth child, Barron Trump, in tow—ten years old at the time of his inauguration in 2017. This was not a typical American presidential family. Donald Trump's five children were born over the span of forty years and three marriages. His oldest three were all grown up with spouses and families of their own. When he was sworn into office, Trump had the second most grandchildren of any American president, a whopping ten, which is tied with George H W Bush but way behind William Henry Harrison's twenty-five.

As First Lady, Melania Trump immediately experienced the vitriol from not only partisan elites of Washington DC—for displacing an entitled Hillary Clinton they believed should have been the First Lady Commander-in Chief—but also from a crazy media that mimicked a tabloid press, concocted drivel and all. She was often targeted by an adversarial press for her fashion sense, or rather her fashion offense toward a press corps that just couldn't accept who she was.

Easily apparent in their backstories, Ivana (the first wife and mother of Trump's first three children), Marla (extra-marital affair turned second wife and mother of daughter Tiffany,) and Melania (First Lady and mother of son Barron) were/are capable mothers and strong, independent women in their own rights, as well as being beautiful and elegant. But since fatherhood tended to take second fiddle to climbing his proverbial ladder, Donald was more than happy to leave the child-rearing and homemaking to the moms while he went off to bring home the bacon.

Showing no hesitation in starting a family, Donald Sr. welcomed his oldest son Donald, Jr. into the world a whopping six days short of nine months after the wedding. Four decades later Trump had accumulated a total of three sons and two daughters, to whom he remains a devoted father (and grandfather to his grandchildren) despite a workaholic nature and constant distractions. Melania continues to be a devoted mother and wife, raising their son Barron as much as possible apart from the hostile political environment in which her husband battles daily, a reality at odds, to say the least, with familial and marital bliss.

Donald Trump is no typical family man, but let's go back and find out what really influenced his matrimonial and paternal habits. His lot in life as a ladies' man is a lock, but a higher order of priorities—namely business and success, the latter measured in terms of deals made, properties owned and dollars in his expanding bank account—meant his early dating life required parental assistance. As a cadet at New York Military Academy, Trump would often be visited on weekends by his dad and mom—Fred and Mary Anne. They would usually be accompanied by a beautiful young woman, a different one each time, occurrences that earned him "Ladies' Man" status in the academy's yearbook, even though it was an all-boys school. Sandy McIntosh, a classmate of Donald's and a witness to this parade of beauties, said that regardless whatever nonverbal message Mr. and Mrs. Trump were delivering to their son, "Our biggest advice in our lives came from Playboy magazine."[1]

More than anything, this teen beauty of the week ploy was part of Mary Anne's attempt to encourage her son to broaden his horizons, to eventually find a girl and settle down, get married and have kids. In short, Donnie needed a wife. Perhaps concerned about what brought Donald to military school in the first place—that wild teenage rebelliousness—Mary Anne might have pushed the matchmaking in hopes of taming that nature. But Donald's ambitions resided elsewhere—with real estate, money, and fame.

It was the summer of 1976, the Bicentennial celebration at full swing in America and the Summer Olympics about to land in neighboring Montreal, when Donald Trump introduced himself to Ivana Zelnicekova Winklmayr. One night around the time of his thirtieth birthday, Trump was out having drinks with Jerry Goldsmith, a private investment banker. They were perched at a Manhattan restaurant and singles bar known as Maxwell's Plum, located at 64th and 1st and owned by Warner LeRoy, son of Mervyn LeRoy, a Hollywood producer of *Wizard of Oz* fame. Maxwell's was a popular watering hole frequented by the celebrity set, among them the Hollywood likes of Barbra Streisand and Warren Beatty. Who could ask for a more appropriate setting for a first encounter between an up-and-coming real-estate billionaire and a long-legged blonde bombshell from Czechoslovakia now residing in Montreal? Ivana and several other models had come to New York to model in a fur show while also promoting the Olympic Games just weeks away.

For a high-profile bachelor like Trump, Maxwell's that night was a target-rich environment for food and frolic, and, from a woman's point a view, the place to be to meet good-looking guys loaded with greenbacks and plenty of heavyweight plastic. Bars like this were as familiar as home to Trump. He frequently mingled and rubbed shoulders with the beautiful people in the city that never sleeps. It wasn't long before Trump got a good look at those long, athletic gams and hazel eyes of a dolled-up, twenty-seven-year-old Ivana. She wasn't just good sport in a social sense but quite sporty. A top-notch alpine skier (her specialties were slalom and downhill), she had been vying, several years earlier and ultimately unsuccessfully, for a spot on the Czech national team, with a dream of racing in the Winter Olympic Games.

"There were lots of pretty girls around, but right away Donald latched onto Ivana," Goldsmith said.[2] "The Donald," as Ivana would later call him, went right to work. She had recently divorced her way out of a brief marriage of convenience having to do with passports, and was now living in Montreal with a longtime boyfriend George Syrovatka, a fellow Czech and competitive skier with whom she had been close for a number of years. Trump reserved a table for Ivana and her friends and he picked up their tab at the end of the night. The next day he sent her a dozen roses, followed a few weeks later by a jaunt to Montreal to visit her and take in a fashion show while there. Soon, Ivana was back in New York, spotted around town riding in a silver limo with the license plate "DJT." Trump brought her to Jamaica Estates to meet his parents, Fred and Mary Anne, and Trump's full-court press on Ivana was underway.

Despite being born on different continents and growing up speaking different tongues, Donald and Ivana were remarkably in sync with one another on a number of levels; both were abundantly self-confident, had been raised by strong fathers, had laser-sharp business acumen, placed great importance in bonds among family members, and enjoyed the sporting life—Donald with his love and skill for golf, and Ivana with her world-class skiing. Trump soon was referring to Ivana as "his twin as a woman." And wherever he went with her—referring to her often as "Ivaska"—he would proclaim to anyone close enough to hear him, "Isn't she gorgeous? Have you ever seen anyone more beautiful?"[3]

Less than a year later Donald and Ivana were married, the wedding taking place in Manhattan's Marble Collegiate Church April 9, the day before Easter 1977. The service was officiated by renowned minister, author, and champion-of-positivity Norman Vincent Peale. Ivana gave birth to their first child, Donald Trump Jr., on New Year's Eve 1977. Donald Jr. was later followed by Ivanka (birth name "Ivana"), born in October 1981, and then Eric, the youngest of Donald and Ivana's three children together, born in early January 1984.

Donald Trump had firmly established himself as his own man and a New York City business icon—well out from under the shadow of his father. He had taken over the family business in 1971 and renamed it the Trump Organization two years later, in 1973. Even with the support of nannies, Ivana dived into motherhood, carving out ample time to be with the three kids. She was the true disciplinarian in the family. But she also devoted her time to frequently being onsite to help her husband in his building of hotels and casinos.

Never content to sit behind a desk, she would often show up at job sites, smartly dressed in designer clothes and spike heels and wearing a hard hat, a clipboard in hand. Described as aggressive and inexperienced in her supervisory/support role, Ivana nonetheless drew praise from her husband. Donald, a stickler for details, was pleased that his wife was an extra set of eyes and ears at worksites ("a natural manager" he once called her).[4] While Trump has an eye for tall, beautiful women (each of his three wives is 5-foot-8 or taller, with modeling or pageant experience), he likes them savvy and independent as well, as also evidenced by his subsequent marriages to Marla Maples and Melania Knauss.

"Mom was tough. She does not put up with nonsense, and I love that about her," younger son Eric Trump said. "I think her toughness is her greatest trait. She's also elegant, charming, and funny. Her personality spans a wide spectrum. There are a lot of people who may be charming but may not be as demanding."[5]

Donald has never been a doting dad, but even as a workaholic he has managed to squeeze in time for his kids, even if it meant their best bet to see him was to drop by his office, where he typically allowed them an open door, even during meetings and important telephone calls. But cutting out of work for hours at a time to catch a Little League game, school play, or dance recital rarely happened. As Donald Jr. said:

> If we wanted to see him, we could see him. If we called, he could be in the middle of the most important meeting, he'd take the phone call. If we wanted to show up in his office, we could play trucks while he's dealing with the biggest guys in banking finance. We'd be making noise, and he was totally fine with it.[6]

But tossing a football or baseball around in the backyard, or a driveway game of hoops one-on-one or H-O-R-S-E? That wasn't going to happen. At dinner time, it was usually Mom with the three kids, and two or three times a week Dad would join them at the table. Once the kids were done eating, Dad and Mom would head out to dinner, frequently as part of social functions.

"We'd talk with him (at dinner time)," Donald Jr. said, "but he'd also be talking with my mother about business. He was good with the kids. He would joke and he'd wrestle with us, but it was for five minutes." In answer to a question if his dad ever yelled at the kids, the younger Donald added, "He got me good once. He was often the instigator. Putting my brother and sister [on the floor] and letting them fight. He'd sit there and laugh, and my mother would have to come in with her Eastern European accent and stop it. He'd get us wound up, then call in my mother to clean up the mess."[7]

When interviewed on late-night television by Conan O'Brien on March 16, 2007, Ivanka, then twenty-five and still single, said of her father,

> He's definitely not a typical father . . . (yet) he was the most accessible dad. He was always there. I would call him in the office . . . he'd have heads of state sitting in the office, and he would put me on speaker phone and tell them how great I was doing in school when I was around nine years old.

The fact is that all four of Donald Trump's four grown children (including Tiffany Trump, the only child Donald and Marla Maples Trump had in their six years of marriage), are highly educated and accomplished in their own right. Yet all have remained close to their dad, even if just emotionally at times, while also working alongside him.

"Truthfully, I was a much better father than I was a husband, always working too much to be the husband my wives wanted me to be," Trump wrote in his 2015 book *Great Again*, right around the time he announced he was seeking the presidency. "I blame myself. I was making my mark in real estate and business, and it was very hard for a relationship to compete with that aspect of my life."[8]

Donald got no argument from Ivana when it was her turn to give her side in her own book, where she wrote about her ex-husband's merits as a father to their three kids. "Donald might not have been the greatest husband to me, but he was a good father to the kids," she said. "Obviously, they adore him and are fiercely loyal to him. If he were a horrible dad, that would not be the case."

Justifiably, Ivana used her published soap box to extol her own skills and virtues as a fulltime working mom. During her fourteen-year marriage to Donald, as she illustrates, she designed the interiors of the Grand Hyatt and Trump Tower, served as president and CEO of the Trump Castle casino (presumably, she opines, the world's only woman in such a role at the time) as well as president and CEO of the Plaza Hotel, the latter position connected to her being named Hotelier of the Year in 1990. That's in addition to writing three international best sellers and raking in tens of millions of dollars with her own lines of fashion, fragrances, and jewelry. She was ambitious and aggressive and successful in an industry dominated by men. And successful motherhood took no back seat to her as a business professional.

"No matter how busy I was," Ivana said, "I had breakfast with my children every day. I sat with them at dinner every night and helped them with their homework (I loved algebra), before going out in a Versace gown to a rubber-chicken charity event. Donald and I celebrated, traveled, and grieved together."[9]

Financial problems put a serious fiscal crimp in the Trump Organization in the latter half of the 1980s. The double whammy for the luxury-loving Ivana came when she found out about Donald's not-so-secret affair with the gorgeous Georgia-born Marla Maples. The 1984 Miss Georgia USA runner-up had 37-25-37 measurements that clearly caught Donald Trump's wandering eye. She was also young, seventeen years his junior.

Donald tried his best to keep his relationship with Marla quiet, but he had a hard time avoiding the prying, opportunistic tabloid press. Meanwhile, Donald's hand-built empire was fraying and in danger of toppling. He was living a life of excessive risk and lies accompanied by piles of debts, looming bankruptcies, adulterous actions, and, as Blair puts it, "overcommitted resources." The casinos, most visibly, were coming up snake eyes, not generating even enough revenue to pay for themselves, let alone turn a profit.

Weathering the business financial storm was par for the Trump course, but "There was one thing he was unable to do—tell his wife (Ivana) it was over," Blair says.

> "I have to confess," he later wrote, "I never sat down calmly with Ivana to 'talk it out' as I probably should have." Nor was his wife able to face squarely the disintegrating situation in which she was living. Meanwhile, Marla Maples was growing tired of being sequestered, of hiding in the back of the limo, of bringing her own escort to public events and standing across the room from her lover, of having a vacation with him mean (having to) travel separately and staying at a different hotel.[10]

Donald was not confrontational when it came to the women in his life. His inability or unwillingness to face reality and command the situation (a tact his business side would have relished) allowed fate and others to determine the success or failure of his matrimonial future.

The duo of duels, one between Donald and Ivana and the other between Ivana and Marla, came to a much-publicized head during Christmas 1989. After flying his family out to Aspen, Colorado, where they stayed in a luxury hotel, he retrieved Marla in a separate trip to also bring her along to Aspen, where she holed up with a girlfriend in more modest quarters several blocks away from the luxury hotel where Ivana and the kids were.

Trump succeeded in keeping his wife and mistress apart for the better part of a week, although Marla and Ivana eventually met up on the same parcel of a ski slope on New Year's Eve (which was also the birthday of Trump's son, Donald Jr.). No doubt Ivana could have challenged Marla and smoked her in a downhill race to the ski lodge, but instead chose to stay and confront Maples, warning her younger rival to stay away from Donald. Ivana punctuated her point with a slight shove of Marla—a moment captured by photographers—for added weight in making her point. "Are you happy?" Maples asked Ivana before they went their separate ways.[1]

* * *

It was just after midnight, early morning on November 9, 2016, and the scene inside New York City's Javits Center was a mixture of tension, anger, and dejection, as if something—or someone (Hillary Clinton maybe?)—were about to explode. The Clinton campaign had rented the Javits Center for what they were confident was going to be Hillary's victory party on Election Night. Yet here it was 12:30 a.m. and the presidential race between her and Donald Trump had not yet been called. And that was bad—no, shocking—news for Hillary, her campaign people, the Democratic Party, and much of the media that had been poised to celebrate a Hillary election as America's first female president.

In the media room, however, word came that Trump had won yet another key battleground state. He was edging closer to the 270 electoral votes he needed to beat Clinton and claim a prize that she believed was rightfully hers. When the announcement came of another state victory for Trump, some reporters in Javits angrily slammed their tables—as reported by a Hollywood Reporter correspondent onsite. Stunned "victory party" guests quietly filed out of the venue, with Hillary supporters muttering "heartbroken," "disappointed," "confused," and "in shock" to describe their feelings as they headed out the door. 12

This much was clear: In winning the U.S. presidency, Trump had assured himself that his next four years and two months—including the gap between his election victory and Washington D.C. inauguration—would see a steady stream of criticism, second-guessing, and mocking from a left-leaning media. The trickle-down was that his family members would also be caught in a frenzy of guilt by association (and party affiliation). That, of course, included Trump's third wife, Melania, whom he had married in January 2005 and was now set to become America's First Lady. It also included their son, Barron, ten years old at the time his father moved into the White House.

Not only was Melania (Knauss) Trump just the second First Lady to have been born outside the USA (Louisa Adams was the first), she was the first who had been an immigrant to the U.S. and the first for whom English was not her first language. It was, in fact, the fifth language in which she is reportedly fluent; she also speaks French, Italian, and German, in addition to her native Slovenian.[13] The fact that she was also a former supermodel with enviable fashion tastes—indisputably one of the most beautiful women in the world—and married to the much-hated Donald Trump gave the media its journalistic license to take aim at Melania. Unlike her predecessor, Michelle Obama, who had been practically worshipped by much of the media, Melania gave the press two public figures (herself and

Donald) for the price of one. In the media world, some of the most prominent public figures get preferential treatment, and some, like the Trumps, don't. Melania has often been the subject of controversy, and some of that controversy was engineered by the media.

Media disrespect toward Melania ramped up a notch or two after her husband declared his presidential candidacy, even before her husband had won the election. One media organization that climbed aboard the anti-Melania train early on was the *Daily Mail*, a British tabloid newspaper that in August 2016 published an article that claimed Melania had worked for an escort service during her days as a model. Mrs. Trump filed suit against the Daily Mail and settled with the newspaper for a judgment of $2.9 million, with the newspaper retracting the story and admitting its falsehood.[14]

Her modeling past also became a source of controversy when it was found she had been part of a sexually explicit photo shoot in the January 1996 issue of a French men's magazine[15] as well as a cover photo for the January 2000 edition of GQ magazine. For the latter, she had posed nude except for diamond jewelry she wore while posing in a reclining position on fur—in Trump's custom-fitted Boeing. Of course, both photo shoots took place more than fifteen years before Trump won the 2016 election and more than five years before they were even married. Donald Trump defended his wife's professional past, saying, "Melania was one of the most successful models, and she did many photo shoots, including for covers and major magazines . . . In Europe, pictures like this are very fashionable and common."[16]

Around the same time of the appearance of the *Daily Mail* story, Melania was accused of plagiarism when the speech she gave at the 2016 Republican National Convention reportedly included a paragraph similar in wording to a segment of Michelle Obama's speech at the 2008 Democratic Convention. A Trump speechwriter later took responsibility for the "confusion." Another charge of plagiarism made against Melania concerning a booklet that had accompanied her Be Best public awareness campaign, was found by fact-checking website Snopes to be "mostly false."[17]

Melania believes she is the most bullied person in the world, but she also admits to having thick enough skin to rarely let herself show her consternation.[18] Melania and Donald are very different in some ways. She is quiet, cautious, and mannered, to her husband's loud, impulsive, and crude. But as a target of partisan venom, they are alike—two peas in the same persnickety political pod.

Other digs against the First Lady have been groundless, a distortion of facts, or simply taking her to task for such meaningless "indiscretions" as discussing certain topics and not others during an interview in which someone else, not Melania, was asking the questions.

Case in point: CNN contributor Kate Anderson Brower opined in a December 2018 commentary that Melania "doesn't understand what it means to be First Lady." Brower's beef with Trump concerned an interview with Fox News's Sean Hannity in which Melania stated that "opportunists who are using my name" was one of the most difficult parts of being First Lady. Brower griped that Melania, at that moment, should have instead been talking about the struggles of Americans she had met in her role as First Lady, such as women and babies dealing with opioid addiction.[19]

Welcome to *All in the First Family*.

Chapter Six

In All Honesty

"You can fool some of the people all of the time, and all of the people some of the time, but you can't fool all of the people all of the time."

-Attributed to Lincoln, but never contemporaneously quoted, during his Bloomington, Illinois, speech on May 29, 1956

TRUMP HAS A KNACK FOR TELLING IT LIKE IT IS. TO SAY WHAT YOU mean in the political arena is not exactly customary of public office seekers. Measured and sanitized responses always beat impulsive slips of the tongue—at least they used to. The year 2015 brought a promising field of presidential hopefuls to challenge the new normal. Round after round of rock'em, sock'em political roughhousing dominated the most unusual nine months in modern American political memory. And the last man standing became the most unlikely champion of the Republican Party. He was a fighter who would charge fearlessly at even the most absurd questions meant to take him down. It gives one pause to wonder what made the people place so much trust in this bulldozer of a candidate.

An anxious American public took sides in 2016 and watched as freedom of speech made a comeback at the same time censorship spiked. Trump began punching the politically correct culture with the energy and aggression of a prizefighter, and he hasn't stopped. He spoke his mind in the political fray with a transparency cheered by masses ready for a little more honesty and a lot less double-talk. The stubborn grip of Trump to the mantra "A promise made must be kept" endeared him to an American people worn out by disappointment and desperate for a different kind of hope and change.

The old adage "The truth hurts" does not seem to apply to Donald Trump. It doesn't seem to hurt him, at least. He tells it like it is, shooting straight, which is a bold concept most politicians shy away from. That's why a populist such as Trump has so many people drawn to him. His appeal is grounded in straight-shooting truth, telling people what they need to hear even if it's not always what they want to hear.

Trump refuses to be stifled by political correctness. That sets him apart from career politicians who are skilled in expressing themselves through carefully selected speech that sounds good and doesn't say anything. The truth hurts? Much of what Trump says is painful to those who don't like him, or at least to those who still resent him for winning an election he wasn't "supposed" to win. The truth according to Trump has several interpretations, or versions, than can be neatly rolled up into one tidy statement. If he offends anyone, that's their problem, not his.

Another way of looking at the conundrum we call Donald Trump is that he believes he is telling the truth even when, technically, he isn't—such as when he's exaggerating or expressing opinions, assessments, achievements, etc. through the art of hyperbole. To his detractors—and they are many, numbering in the millions—all those types of statements get categorized as lies. To his supporters—and there are many, too, numbering in the millions—they are not to be taken literally; they only represent the kind of big talk commonly spoken by common people, and not to be taken too seriously. With Trump, we get the point.

For example, in giving an inventory of his accomplishments in his first couple years of his presidency, Trump said that he had "enacted the biggest tax cuts and reforms in American history." He lobbed another log onto the fire when he said that "our economy is the strongest it's ever been in the history of our country."[1] A fact check shows that the first of those two Trump brags was statistically incorrect—the tax cuts and reforms were actually the eighth-largest. The bit about the economy wasn't yet true at the time (it was spoken in 2018), although it might have been true or close to true a little over a year later, by early 2020, just before the COVID-19 pandemic hit U.S. shores.

But was any of that really lying—being untruthful by its very definition? It depends. Like anything else going on in America that could be construed as political, it's in the ear of the beholder. If you belonged to that half of the American populace that detested Trump, then what Trump said in those statements of achievement were a nasty lie; if you were in the other approximately half of the nation that remained loyal to Trump, you would call it speaking the truth in the sense that the gist of what he's saying feels true. Such tax cuts and reforms had been a long time coming; even if the indicators didn't exactly match up with certain unprecedented thresholds.

The economy sure felt like it was the best it had been in a very long time. That's what Trump was implying, using words that were already on the minds of many Americans. We get it; we were doing pretty darn well economy-wise as a country, with unemployment figures reaching the lowest they had been in many years, and the stock market continuing to reach new highs. At worst, the economy was doing just fine; a whole lot better than in the wake of the recession of 2008-09, barely ten years earlier.

In his bestselling book *The Art of the Deal*, written decades before his election, Trump gave an honest preview of what America would see with him as president.

> The final key to the way I promote is bravado. I play to people's fantasies. People may not always think big themselves, but they can still get very excited by those who do. That's why a little hyperbole never hurts. People want to believe that something is the biggest and the greatest and the most spectacular. I call it truthful hyperbole. It's an innocent form of exaggeration—and a very effective form of promotion.[2]

This is Trump's way of keeping it real, even if what he says isn't the factual truth. Trump isn't your run-of-the-mill politician speaking a politician's version of "shooting straight." He is quite clearly a nonpolitician speaking a nonpolitical brand of straight talk.

Trump is an outsider who broke into the inner circle of Washington, DC's politically powerful elite, most of whom—when you count some of his fellow Republicans—clearly don't want him there. He is an outlier, which Merriam-Webster defines as "a person or thing that is atypical within a particular group, class, or category." Even among the politically incorrect, Trump is politically incorrect. And he knows it. He says what he means, and it doesn't come out filtered. He'll say it to crowds at rallies, and he'll say it to media members, knowing that in many cases those reporters will cherry pick his statements out of context or twist the meanings of his words to make them fit into a liberal narrative that often sounds like nothing Trump has actually said or written. Yet, Trump soldiers on, being who he is. A fly in the ointment of the Washington elite.

Millions of Americans continue to applaud this president who is all about going against the grain—and speaking the truth. Keeping it real.

"The fact is I give people what they need and deserve to hear—exactly what they don't get from politicians—and that is The Truth," Trump said in his 2016 book *Great Again*, a paperback originally published in late 2015 as a hardcover called *Crippled America*.

> Our country is a mess right now, and we don't have time to pretend otherwise. We don't have time to waste on being politically correct . . . I think the big problem this country has is being politically incorrect. I've been challenged by so many people, and I don't frankly have the time for total political correctness . . . What I say is what I say, and everyone that knows me really appreciates it. [3]

One of the most telling portrayals of Trump as a truth merchant was told by *Washington Post* columnist Marc A. Thiessen. In 2018, a little more than a year and a half into Trump's first term, Thiessen wrote that Trump might be remembered as the most honest U.S. president in American history, while conceding that "Trump lies all the time." It is a total contradiction, and yet it isn't, which deserves an explanation from Thiessen, who has often appeared as a guest on Fox News:

> "In part, it's a New York thing—everything is the biggest and the best," Thiessen wrote in a Post column entitled "Trump Could Be the Most Honest President in Modern History." But when it comes to the real barometer of presidential truthfulness—keeping his promises—Trump is a paragon of honesty. For better or worse, since taking office Trump has done exactly what he promised he would. [4]

Thiessen backs up this seeming stumper of analysis, rattling off numerous examples of how Trump had fulfilled promises he made while campaigning for office during the last few months of 2015 and through the election in November 2016. Thiessen cites things such as Trump's fulfillment of a pledge to move the U.S. embassy in Israel from Tel Aviv to Jerusalem, something which all three of his immediate predecessors had been unable to do. He also points out that Trump established and enforced bans on travel to the United States from countries deemed as havens for international terrorists, as promised. Further, Trump nominated and won appointments for Supreme Court justices who would fit the Constitutional mold of Justice Antonin Scalia (those turned out to be Neil M. Gorsuch, Brett M. Kavanaugh and Amy Coney Barrett), just as he had promised. And finally, Trump followed through on introducing and securing Congressional passage of historic tax reforms that included the first significant revamping of the U.S. tax code in decades. [5]

"Whether one agrees or disagrees is not the point," Thiessen says.

"When Trump says he will do something, you can take it to the bank. Yes, he takes liberties with the truth. But unlike his predecessor (Barack Obama), he did not pass his signature legislative achievement on the basis of a lie ('If you like your health-care plan, you can keep it.')—which is clearly worse than falsely bragging that your tax cut is the biggest ever.

The fact is, in his first two years, Trump has compiled a remarkable record of presidential promise-keeping. He'd probably say it's the best in history—which may or may not end up being true. It's too soon to tell.[6]

Trump has admitted he is a man that the media loves to hate. In part, that's because he fights back. Go after him with criticisms and accusations and if he believes these are false charges or incorrect reporting to add to the anti-Trump narrative—what he calls "fake news," a term that Trump has cemented in the American lexicon—if he believes you're adding to the lies, you'll get another dose of Trump counterpoint delivered, usually via Twitter or a direct callout in his next news conference. Trump never seems to tire of this incessant volleying between himself and members of the media, not for the sport of it, but for the purpose of pointing out where the news has steered itself wrong.

Trump also refuses to accept any poll that paints him, his policies, or his promises in a negative or false light. If nothing else, he has motivated, even forced, media in general to take heightened responsibility for its conduct and accuracy of reporting. If you're looking for Trump to follow unwritten rules about what a president's decorum or limits of brash talk should be, you can forget about it. Not with him. Again, he refuses to use filters to appease anyone who is looking for him to engage in any of the traditional doublespeak or carefully crafted talking points . . . like those spewed by traditional politicians (and there are many) who would rather camouflage their commentary than speak the unvarnished truth of whatever convictions they might have.

Trump has said,

It hasn't taken me long to learn how truly dishonest the political media can be. . . . I'm perhaps a controversial person; I say what's on my mind. I don't wait to hear what a pollster has to say because I don't use pollsters. The media loves my candor. They know I'm not going to dodge or ignore their questions. I have no problems telling it like it is.[7]

Telling it like it is—that's Trump's forte. If he says he's going to do something, he forges ahead on it. "Trump promised to cancel President Barack Obama's Clean Power plan, withdraw from the Paris climate accord, approve the Keystone XL and Dakota Access pipelines, and open the Arctic National Wildlife Refuge to exploration," Thiessen writes. "He fulfilled all of those pledges." [8]

Critics have castigated Trump for having the gall to cancel programs or undo policies and executive orders put in place by his predecessor, Barack Obama. It is not the content or agenda of these programs and policies themselves that have stuck in the craw of Trump's political enemies—it is the fact they consider his presidency an illegitimate one because he lost the national popular vote, even though he won the electoral vote, which by constitutional law determines the outcome. Anti-Trumpsters have been taking it out on him ever since, persistently calling him a "liar," a "racist," and a "misogynist," and attempting to discredit and twist his words at every opportunity.

Trump stays firm against these attacks:

The most important lesson in this—stand behind your word, and make sure your word stands up. People who have done business with me will tell you that I never say something unless I mean it.

I don't make promises I can't keep. I don't make threats without following through. Don't ever make the mistake of thinking you can bully me.[9]

Even when the media steps in to assist the anti-Trumpers, Trump circumvents the process like no other prominent public official before him. If the media—like CNN reporter Jim Acosta, a master at baiting and bashing Trump—goes on the offensive, Trump often resorts to Twitter to get his words out, unvarnished and untwisted, straight to the American people, love him or hate him.

"He is able to communicate directly to the people over the heads of the media, to make sure the people know what's going on, the work that he's doing," political pundit Tammy Bruce said, during a January 2020 interview with Peter Varney of Fox News.

"This is a man that, for the first time ever, we've seen a president who is so transparent and consistent in who he is, what his attitude has been. You don't see this man changing; you don't have to wonder if he is telling you the truth. You might not like it necessarily, all the time, but you know that you can trust him . . . that he's telling you honestly what the situation is."[10]

It has been interesting to watch and read how the media reacts to the answers Trump gives, whether those answers are honest or evasive. For example, Trump gave a sit-down interview outside the White House with Fox News's Chris Wallace on a steamy day in July 2020. Truth in reporting is as important as what comes out of the mouth of the American president, and, in dealing with Trump, this is where the media often falls short. Some post-interview accounts described Trump as drenched in sweat ("flop sweat"). In fact, you could watch the interview and see some sweat on Trump's face, mostly limited to the small area between his nose and upper lip, and dabs of it high on his cheeks, but nothing that resembled true flop sweat. (Think of Albert Brooks's news reporter character in the movie *Broadcast News,* getting his disastrous shot as a nightly news anchor.)

Late in the interview, Wallace asked Trump if he would be a good loser if he were to lose the 2020 election. Trump admitted he isn't a good loser, and that he rarely loses, but that his concern for 2020 was that widespread mail-in voting would be rigged. He was referring to the belief of many conservative-leaning voters that mail-in voting—mentioned prominently as an alternative to in-person voting at polling places because of the lingering effects of the coronavirus pandemic—would leave voting vulnerable to corrupt voting practices. Wallace then asked Trump, "Are you saying you might not accept the results of the election? . . . I asked you the same question at [one of Trump's three 2016 debates against Democrat challenger Hillary Clinton]."

"I will tell you at the time; I will keep you in suspense," Trump said. "You know, she (Clinton) is the one who never accepted (her loss in 2016). She never accepted her loss, and she looks like a fool."[11]

In being noncommittal on the issue of accepting the election result, Trump drew the wrath of many in the media and many more on social media, interpreting his comments to Wallace to mean that he would refuse to leave the White House. That he would need to be taken out of office by some show of force. This is the world in which we live, in the 2020s—with words being twisted at every turn.

Trump was being forthright, expressing his honest, reasonable feelings—that indeed he might have something to say about it if evidence shows that there are irregularities in voting. Why wouldn't he? Presumably, his Democrat opponent would do the same thing. After all, we saw what happened after the 2016 election; Robert Mueller was appointed a special counsel to investigate speculation there had been collusion between the Russians and Trump's campaign. Further, Clinton bashed the Electoral College (mandated by the U.S. Constitution) and hopped from one election-related accusation to another, blaming a variety of factors for her unaccepted loss (unexpected to her, the Democratic National Committee, and much of the media). She even wrote a book about it.

One important thing about Trump is how he deals in honesty. He's not a politician; he's a businessman, and he speaks and acts without a filter. For decades Washington D.C. needed an outsider to come in and speak plainly without a concern for appeasing people or acting "presidential." Someone who would appeal to, and make his appeals to, the common man and woman—people he could connect with by speaking to them about what was on his mind, to include his likes and dislikes. He's not a polished politician spouting talking points, but instead making credible points with a refreshing air about him, being a bit rough around the edges.

"Donald Trump might not have been the perfect candidate, but he was ours," Trump photographer Gene Ho writes in *Trumpography*. "He took to the podium, with a mic and the gumption, to give us the gross, honest truth. It was raw and unpolished. And in those glorious flaws came a truth that unraveled while we were waking: 'A flawed man fighting for what's right is any man fighting for what's right.'"[12]

Trump doesn't weigh or mince his words before speaking them; he says what's on his mind and he's loaded with opinions, most of them better supported than what his detractors give him credit for. If you don't like what he says, that is one hundred percent your problem. And he reacts like we do to things that we see and hear. When National Football League football players started taking a knee during the national anthem, Trump said if he were in charge, he would fire them. It was a statement for which he got blistered by a left-leaning media sympathetic toward players disrespecting the flag and their fans, especially those who had served their country. Trump's critics take unrelenting potshots at him, devising every trick in the book to try and get him out of office. Like when a Democrat-led House of Representatives passed articles of impeachment against him when at least half of America knew the impeachment premise was a political sham and procedural sham. Since then, political hits have been bombarding Trump from all directions, most landing below the belt.

When Trump gets ready to open his mouth or grab his mobile device to tweet or post, the media is poised to pounce. On a good day, they will also report.

About a month after his election in 2016, Trump took a phone call from the Taiwanese president, sending those in the federal intelligence and foreign affairs sectors into a tizzy. They were horrified, believing that the newly elected U.S. president-to-be was, in effect, thumbing his nose at China. For many years Chinese officials had demanded of America that we not recognize Taiwan as a sovereign entity. By taking the phone call, the media reported, Trump was violating a diplomatic tradition with China, not a superpower that we want to cross swords with, not even in a diplomatic sense.

Amid the angry, overwrought protests that came Trump's way, he tweeted out, "Interesting how the U.S. sells Taiwan billions of dollars of military equipment, but I should not accept a congratulatory call."

In fact, it had been a call that had been scheduled months earlier. One of the orders of business turned out to be the offer of congratulations to Trump for his election victory, surely not a sentiment worthy of setting off World War III. And yet, it is conceded that in accepting the call and engaging in conversation with his Taiwanese counterpart, Trump was demonstrating that a new era had arrived in U.S.-China relations, one that would not necessarily adhere to past policies.

To much of the world beyond the city limits of Washington, D.C., such pragmatism on the part of Trump was quite reasonable, it made sense. It was real world, not another dose of abstract appeasement typically accompanied by a dangerous dance around the core issues. [13] The hard part was explaining all this to a media that is at its best when it exercises healthy cynicism, but that's not the tact much of the media takes with Trump. Even before he came up with the phrase "fake news" to describe efforts made by news outlets in some of their reportage of Trump and the nation in general, the media hound dogs were already in a left-leaning, combative mode looking for whatever "gotcha" material they could dig up--or make up. This type of cynicism is not a matter of poking through the talking points to find out the truth behind them; it's taking pokes at a president that was unwilling to acquiesce to the politically correct narrative.

"The other thing I do when I talk with reporters is to be straight," Trump said. "I try not to deceive them or to be defensive, because those are precisely the ways most people get themselves into trouble with the press."[14] Trouble, it turned out, was the goal--trouble for Trump. Their maniacal desire was to hound and badger him into awkward or damning positions. Without missing a beat, Donald Trump would verbally veer off the trail and decisively deflect the intended blow.

Honesty isn't just about truth—whether spoken or borne out through one's actions—it's about integrity. It's about being a person of conviction, doing the right thing when no one is watching, and following through on a promise. It has to be developed and nurtured faithfully over the years, long before reaching the public eye. That's how Trump described it, speaking of his own life long before he entered politics.

> When I went into business for myself, I made it a point to establish a reputation that bankers and other professionals would be comfortable with, and I knew that eventually my integrity as a businessman would be intact. People are more apt to want to work with you if they feel they can trust you.[15]

Trump isn't phony; he's blunt but he's plainspoken, easily understood by the simplest American citizen. But his detractors and obsessive second-guessers let their hate and disdain toward him color how they interpret his speeches, interviews, Truth Social posts, etc. When Trump exaggerated the size of the crowd at his January 2017 inauguration, they proclaimed him a liar. Just as they did with a myriad other things he said or wrote.

What Trump actually has is a no-nonsense approach to life and the presidency that sounds perfectly reasonable and sensible to anyone living outside of or not brainwashed by the political speak that permeates life and corrupted thinking all along the Potomac. This political posturing produced an environment of posturing and pandering that masquerades as statesmanship. But not in Trump's world. As former House Speaker Newt Gingrich puts it in *Understanding Trump,*

> Trump wants to set aside the abstract establishment theories and get to what makes up the real world. In a way, I would argue that Trump's way of thinking is a reversion to Tocqueville, Lincoln, and

Washington. If you look at the original American system, it was extraordinarily fact-based.[16]

Robert Kiyosaki, best-selling author of *Rich Dad, Poor Dad,* and a friend of Trump's, sees the forty-fifth president as consistently straight to the point and truthful, even when it hurts.

> In most instances, his thoughts, words, and actions are the same. Maybe this is why he is direct and blunt. He can be blunt because his thoughts, words, and actions are integrated, congruent, acting as one. Many of us know people who are, actually, three people. They think one thing, say something else, and do not do what they say or think.[17]

Trump doesn't let a crowd's occasional negative reactions to something he said dissuade him from saying it. When he campaigned on a number of pledges he would bring to the presidency, some of them entailing reversals of policies and executive orders issued by his predecessor, Barack Obama. Those included building a wall along the Mexican border to thwarting illegal immigrants to repealing Obamacare (one of his few unsuccessful goals). He sticks to his guns despite an opposition that impeached him in a failed attempt to remove him from office, and continue to try to knock him out of the political arena. When he's wrong—in his judgment, not someone else's—he will backtrack, just as he did when he ultimately abandoned a plan to completely pull U.S. forces out of Afghanistan. While Trump has bent the truth at times, it's nothing compared to the outright fibs of Obama, whose signature legislative victory—one that gave us Obamacare—was based on a blatant lie ("If you like your health-care plan, you can keep it.") Obama also lied in his explanation for what caused the terrorist attack on the U.S. embassy in Benghazi, resulting in the deaths of four Americans. And Biden follows suit with whoppers like "The economy is great!" and "What border crisis?"

When he first ran for president in 2016, Trump needed the backing of Christian evangelicals. It was an endorsement he quickly won, despite his personal baggage that included two failed marriages, one known illicit affair (Marla Maples), and accusations, albeit unproven, of at least one affair with a porn actress—Stephanie "Stormy Daniels" Clifford. What ultimately sold Trump to the Christian base was his authenticity, a quality long admired by evangelicals who fully understood the concepts of forgiveness and redemption. "President Trump represented to the evangelical community a warrior to fight the encroachment of the federal government in their lives and in their institutions," the *Washington Post's* Robert Costa wrote.

> "In a sense they forgave him for all his personal misdeeds because they believed he could be a strong man in taking away regulations or different federal guidelines that they saw as a burden for their church, or for their religious institutions."[18]

Texas-based evangelist James Robison, a friend of Trump's, is among millions who cherish his "give it to me straight" philosophy on life, business, and politics. One of the things Robison told Trump during the latter's presidential campaign in 2016 was to avoid using religious terminology in public discourse. Robison knew it might come across as phony and hurt his election chances. "It'll backfire," Robison said he told Trump. And "he did it. He never tried to prove to you or anybody else he's a great spiritual giant. I made it clear that he was growing in his faith. But here's what he knew. 'I can't win without evangelicals and professing Christians.'"[19]

In his commitment to authenticity, Trump reveals a pet peeve: hypocrisy. He has a sincere aversion to it, and that includes the treatment of Christians in America. "I don't understand why the same people who demand respect for their beliefs often don't show respect for the beliefs of others," Trump has said. "It seems like every week there is a negative ruling on some issue having to do with Christianity. I think it's outrageous, totally outrageous." [20]

Chapter Seven
American Original

"Always bear in mind that your own resolution to succeed is more important than any other one thing."
-Abraham Lincoln's letter to Isham Reavis, Nov. 5, 1855

WHAT EXACTLY DOES IT MEAN TO BE A SELF-MADE MAN? HORATIO ALGER defined the idea in his nineteenth-century novels as a person who comes up from nothing. His parade of poor, humble characters who rose from the bottom rung of the ladder to become successful and comfortable in life portrayed true rags-to-riches tales. Titles such as *Ragged Dick, Fame and Fortune,* and *Bound to Rise* were devoured by young adults who craved the hopeful storylines and happy endings. An Abraham Lincoln could definitely have played the part of one of Horatio's boys. He rose from poor, hardscrabble farm boy to American president (He even gave it a title: *Annals of the Poor*). But a Donald Trump? How absurd is it to ponder a millionaire's son rising up the ladder—wasn't he already at the top? Maybe that's the question: must one rise from nothing? Perhaps one's poverty or lack thereof may be less significant than how far one rises above that first step.

"Self-invented" or "self-determined" may be better labels for climbers who rise above their initial circumstances by their own stubborn will. Lincoln told young men that "will" was the most important quality for success. Trump wrote a book on it titled *Never Give Up.* And, let's be honest, Alger strategically placed wealthy benefactors along the trail of his poor boys. Perhaps to prove that it takes a village after all. Unearthing those influential helpers perched on the Trump ladder revealed some things: success doesn't happen by chance, and rarely entirely on one's own. Dogged determination and having a village of supporters are certainly steps along the way. But what about energy and ambition, and just plain good fortune?

In truth, many ingredients converge for one human being to make something of himself or herself.

Donald Trump was born into wealth, his father a highly successful developer who was eventually worth more than a quarter billion dollars. Appearances and circumstances reveal little, if anything, in common between Horatio Alger's poor boys and Trump, yet Trump made his way in the world by creating his own opportunities, and, in his own distinct manner, overcame steep odds to become president of the United States.

After all, no one would have thought a thrice-married, prima donna, billionaire businessman who was once embroiled in bankruptcy hell while publicly flogged by a henpecking media—a man without a shred of political experience—would bounce back to be elected to the highest office in the land. And this was after nay-saying pundits nationwide had predicted with near certainty, even just twenty-four hours prior to his win, that he would be defeated at the polls, not worthy of even being on the ballot.

Look at it this way: Trump was a different kind of self-made man. Although the elder Trump was already a wealthy man by the time his fourth child—Donald John—was born in 1946, Fred and Mary Trump had gone to great lengths to shield their five children from the domestic trappings of a wealthy existence.

"We had a very traditional family," Trump wrote in *The Art of the Deal.*

> My father was the power and the breadwinner, and my mother was the perfect housewife . . . We lived in a large house, but we never thought of ourselves as rich kids. We were brought up to know the value of a dollar and to appreciate the importance of hard work.[1]

As a teen and later while in college and immediately after, Donald learned the ropes of the construction business at his father's side. He was still in his twenties when his dad kicked himself upstairs to become chairman of the board, leaving the briefly vacant president's chair to be Donald's. Yet, the younger Trump harbored other ideas; he wanted to be on his own. Not long after consolidating his dad's corporate holdings under one 'umbrella,' now known as the Trump Organization, he went out on his own, moving from the world of Brooklyn and Queens to an almost entirely separate orbit in Manhattan, where, for all practical purposes, Donald would be starting over. It would mean having to deal—and scrap and scrape—among an entirely new slate of movers and shakers.

"He had upscaled his own life as well, with a move to Manhattan's Upper East Side," Gwenda Blair writes in *The Trumps*.

> Settling into a small, dark studio on the seventeenth floor of a twenty-one-floor building, he blithely referred to his new living quarters as a penthouse and began carving out a new life as a debonair bachelor. 'Moving into that apartment was probably more exciting for me than moving, fifteen years later, into the top three floors of Trump Tower,' he wrote later.[2]

The move—both in terms of greater New York City geography and career orientation—was a bit of a mystery to Fred Trump. He had apparently believed that Donnie would inherit the reins of the family business—the only Trump child deemed capable of or otherwise willing to take on such a handed-down responsibility—and stay there for decades to come. Young Trump's itch for the brighter lights and bigger city was too much of a tease for him not to chase Manhattan. "He thought I was crazy," Trump would say of his dad years later. "Nevertheless, he had a confidence in me. I'll never forget when he told my incredible mother, 'Look, I don't know if he is right or wrong, but I've got to let him do it. He has great ability and talent.'"[3]

Trump also said, "I want to be in mid-Manhattan, where all the top stuff is going on. I'll never be involved with the old man's property except when he needs me."[4]

In a coincidental twist, Trump's uptown move was remarkably similar to the story line of a popular 1970s television sitcom spun off from another show. The year that Trump moved out of Queens was the same year that the classic-to-be sitcom *All in the Family* (with politically incorrect Archie Bunker as head of the household) debuted on TV. One set of recurring supporting characters on the show were the Jeffersons, a couple who came into some money and started a cleaning business that quickly became very successful and made them wealthy, inspiring them to leave Queens and make the big move up ("movin' on up") to the East Side of Manhattan—roughly around the same time in real time that Donald Trump was settling into his new digs in the same part of the city.

Author Gene Ho wrote this in extolling Trump's self-made-man virtues in *Trumpography*:

Man is made or unmade by himself. The pursuit of knowledge, experience, understanding, common sense, and insight map the path to wisdom. Still, having a map doesn't guarantee one will arrive at his or her destination. It takes conscious effort and a focused objective to work relentlessly toward personal improvement. Wisdom is not a set destination but found in the journey. Through that journey, the truth boils down to one human philosophy—wisdom comes from living well.[5]

Donald Trump's schooling invariably influenced his future. He had great schooling and educational opportunities starting from age three, although there was still a sense that he was doing things his own way and seeking or creating opportunities for himself outside the norm of the privileged school child. It was at the age of three that he attended Carousel Pre-School, at the time a new nursery program located in Jamaica Estates, not far from home. Carousel's director was Shirley Greene, who had been trained in early childhood education at two prestigious programs, including one conducted at Columbia University, and who had now established what was regarded as a model nursery school in an old house. Described as "avant-garde" for its time (this was the late 1940s), Carousel's focus was on "individual development and hands-on learning experiences from gardening and outdoor play to collecting snowflakes (the kind falling from the sky on wintry days, not persons of an especially lightweight form of liberal political persuasion), and especially building with blocks." Said Greene, "Donald was a beautiful little boy, very blond and buttery. He was a nice size for his age, very attractive, social, and outgoing. He wasn't fat, but he was really sturdy, and really quite jolly."[6]

At age five, Trump was enrolled in Kew Forest, a private school with a more structured environment than Carousel. Students wore mandated school uniforms and sang hymns every morning at assembly. The dress for boys was navy blazer with the school crest on the pocket accompanied by school tie and charcoal-colored pants. Girls wore a white blouse to go with navy blue jumpers. This was Donnie's introduction to discipline and regimentation outside of the home. Over the years it would become evident that with his suave and competitive nature, he enjoyed living outside the rules when possible

It was at Kew Forest that Trump met up with Peter Brant, who likewise came from a wealthy family and would end up being Donald's best friend for many years. Together, they were more than a handful for most teachers and school officials and very similar in terms of comportment (or lack of it), although they were physical opposites—Peter was shorter and chunkier with a darker complexion, while Donnie was tall for his age, with the fair-haired look of a choir boy. Both Peter and Donnie were of above-average intelligence but with below-average grades, apparently saving their energies for outside the classroom, where they excelled as athletes, competing on several teams and winning more than their share of medals and trophies. "Sports was our whole life then," Brant said years later. "We were in our own world."[7]

They were in their own world in more ways than one; the two boys were frequently committing mischief, shooting spitballs and cracking jokes—no doubt attempts to garner attention and get a rise out of teachers. "They were extremely competitive and had to be on top whichever way they could," classmate Fina Farhi Geiger said.

> They really pushed the limits in terms of authority and what they could get away with... We grew up at a time when everyone basically went by the rules, which means being respectful. Peter and Donald didn't do that. They weren't respectful. They did their own thing. Donald was very sharp and knew just what he could get away with.[8]

The tipping point for young Trump came after he and Brant snuck off for an excursion into New York City, with Trump returning home with the switchblade that his parents soon discovered. This is when Fred Trump decided it was time to crack down and send his son, now thirteen, off to military school. He enrolled Donald in New York Military Academy about fifty-five miles north of the city in the small town of Cornwall-on-Hudson, near West Point (the United States Military Academy). Donald's life at the military school was about to smooth off some of his rough edges. No more goofing around.

From the day they arrived, new cadets quickly found themselves drilled and ordered around by higher-ranking upperclassmen. They learned how to march, how to salute, how to perform basic military maneuvers. Often and at random times, they were told to stand at attention and recite academy traditions and rules that they were supposed to memorize. They ran errands at an upperclassman's whim, dropped and knocked out push-ups, ate square meals, and basically did whatever they were told to do, no matter how troublesome or vexing. "It's not an easy task for a boy away from home, having people bark at you, do this, do that, get in step, keep your mouth closed, take a shower, do your homework, go to bed, get up," said Col. Ted "Doby" Dobias, an NYMA graduate and World War II veteran who was a tactical training officer and athletic coach at the school. "Kids would burst into tears and beg to go home."[9]

Not Donald Trump; he was no washout. In fact, he seemed to take everything in stride, doing what he was told, keeping his nose clean, and tolerating academy life better than most boys there. His character was being built. He was learning to be organized. And he seemed to know what he was doing all the time, even when there was a more-senior cadet screaming in his ear that would have made many of his peers cringe. Although he wasn't one of the top overall students in his class, he did okay competing for grades and at one point managed to get the highest grades in geometry.

Trump was drawn to Dobias and sought instruction from the military veteran. This is important to know in unlocking the key to part of Trump's past and understanding why he indeed is a self-made man, not everything handed to him on a silver platter, like a spoiled, entitled real-life version of comic book icon Richie Rich. According to Dobias,

(Trump) caught my eye right away because he was so aggressive but so coachable. Lots of kids you can talk to until you're blue in the face and nothing happens, but Donald would react to instructions. If you told him he wasn't throwing the baseball correctly, he'd do it right the next time. If you said he wasn't blocking a tackle high enough, he'd correct it. He was very sure of himself, but he also listened.[10]

That made Trump an avid learner, willing to put ego aside to accept guidance and correction. He listened and learned, and he adjusted accordingly. These are traits that would serve him well in the business world, where listening is often more important to a negotiation or getting a deal done than talking.

New York Military Academy was all about hierarchy, respect for authority, handling physical and mental duress, and performing under pressure, complete with spit-shined shoes and brilliantly polished brass buckles. Trump didn't just survive those five years there, he thrived. Over time, as Fred and Mary Trump visited him there on occasion, they could see that their son had been transformed.

Something had taken hold of Donald Trump at New York Military Academy and it served him well when he got to college, his first two years at Fordham and his last two at Wharton (the University of Pennsylvania), where he was one of a handful of students who majored in real estate. In majoring in business, he meant business. This was a key component to prepare him for life not only beyond college, but several years later after he had broken away from the family business to stake his own claim in Manhattan. Military school had shaped him up and sharpened his focus on who he was and what he wanted to do with his life. Eventually he would be out on his own before the age of thirty, a secure, well-paying career awaiting him working full-time for his dad if he so chose. He didn't.

By the time he got to Fordham—a Roman Catholic school run by the Jesuits (Trump was not Catholic)—he had matured and had the suave personality liked by both boys and girls, and he was someone who didn't let things bother him. The older cadets at Cornwall-on-Hudson had driven that out of him, apparently. But still, why Fordham? "I'd been away at school (NYMA) for five years, and I wanted to see my parents," Trump said. Asked the same question, though, his sister Maryanne simply said, "It's where he got in."[11]

At Fordham, Trump stood out, and it wasn't just the signs of his family's wealth evidenced in the well-tailored clothes he wore or the expensive red sports car he drove around in. Although the sixties were a time where cigarette smoking was chic and sophisticated, Trump was having none of that. He didn't smoke and he avoided alcohol. When it came to sports, he kept his cool, even in defeat, never smashing his squash racquet after a loss, as did some of his teammates. "He had a certain aura," teammate Rich Marrin said. "He didn't have tantrums, and he was never late. If anything, he was more of a gentleman than we were, more refined, as if brought up in a stricter family, with more emphasis on manners."[12]

Well, there was that one exception when, on a team trip to Washington DC, he pulled a new set of golf clubs out of the back of his car and hit about a half-dozen new balls into the Potomac River, an impulsive yet extravagant exhibition that teammates watching never forgot.

When his sophomore year at Fordham was over, Trump decided it was time to move on to more serious matters—in this case his education, or, more specifically, his business education, his destination Wharton, the University of Pennsylvania's prestigious business school. Because he was a transfer student, Trump wasn't eligible to join any varsity athletics teams at Penn, not that it mattered to him. His top priority was learning, and Wharton had one of the few real estate departments among American colleges and universities.

"For the next two years, Donald and his (five) classmates (all taught by one departmental professor) studied finance, mortgages, accounting, and money and banking," Blair writes.

> Working together in teams, they learned how to analyze neighborhoods and make appraisals by walking around and going into bars to see what ethnic groups were there . . . For Donald it was familiar and welcome territory. For the first time in his life, what he was studying seemed relevant. Finally there was a classroom competition he wanted to win.[13]

Real estate was a language Trump knew and could speak with professional fluency, making him the expert in the class . . . certainly in the eyes of the professor. In Trump, he had a student with whom he could commiserate on real estate matters beyond what was taught and discussed in the classroom. "I remember the professor talking to Donald like one insider to another," said fellow real estate major Peter Gelb. "We were the students, and they were the pros."[14]

Trump was old school in his own way while coming up in the world. He possessed a willingness to work hard, to get down and dirty. Before setting off on his own to build grand hotels and casinos, he was at his father's knee, so to speak, often performing mundane tasks and running errands. These were the sort of "gofer" things that a no-name apprentice—no pun intended—would start out doing at the ground floor in hopes of working his or her way up the ladder.

While still a teenager, Trump worked on the maintenance crew at a foreclosed FHA project—an apartment complex—in Maryland that his father had bought. It was there that Donnie Trump got his hands dirty. "I wore a T-shirt and worked in the machine shop," he would say years later. "I loved it, working with my hands, and I saw a different world, the world of the guys who cleaned and fixed things." Other beginning-level grunt work that young Trump performed included collecting the coins from the washer and dryer machines in the laundry rooms, hosing down dust at the Trump Village construction site, and chauffeuring his father around from one job site or appointment to another. "He was a real eager beaver, a go-getter," Trump Village architect Morris Lapidus said. "Whenever his father gave him something to do, he would be off and running. You could tell that he was going to get somewhere."[15]

Donald Trump, entrepreneur and businessman, mastered a pragmatic approach to self-educating himself on unfamiliar subjects. Case in point when he accepted the challenge to rebuild Wollman Rink in New York City's Central Park. It was a formidable, hot-potato type of task which no one in the city—Mayor Ed Koch included—had been able to figure out. Along came Trump. As a practical businessman familiar with the concept of learning by doing, and having already gone public in criticizing Koch's efforts to rebuild the rink, Trump accepted the exasperated Koch's challenge: six months to build the rink and restrict the cost to $3 million or less. He would rebuild the rink within a strict budget and tight deadline mandated to him, even though he had no experience in knowing what it takes to build a major ice rink.

To get up to speed on the ice rink, Trump didn't check out books from a library. He had a better idea, and that meant aiming north—where the official national pastime was ice hockey. "So Trump decided he needed to talk with someone who was an expert at building skating rinks, which naturally made him think of Canada," Newt Gingrich writes in *Understanding Trump*.

> Ultimately, he got in touch with a Toronto-based company that had built the rink for the Montreal Canadiens hockey team. Trump got a crash course in what it takes to build a quality skating rink, then he had some people from the company to fly down to look at Wollman Rink with him. Within three months, at a cost of $2.25 million, the rink was open for business. It's still there and still making ice (and the Wollman Rink in Central Park continues to be associated with Trump). I love this story because it shows that Trump is a pragmatic, sensible conservative who knows how to finish difficult projects under immense pressure.[16]

Trump is a natural learner, someone who chooses to learn on his own accord, and learn by doing—by not being shy about asking the right questions of the right people. Roger Schank, of the Institute for the Learning Sciences at Northwestern University, says that people learn by doing the things that they want to do. On his website he says, "Learning occurs when someone wants to learn, not when someone wants to teach." Schank is the author of a study titled "What We Learn When We Learn by Doing," which is referenced by Newt Gingrich in his book *Understanding Trump:*

> To consider learning by doing from a psychological point of view, we must think more about learning in real life, which is, of course, the natural venue of learning by doing. There is, after all, something inherently artificial about school. Natural learning means learning on an 'as needed' basis. In such a learning situation, motivation is never a problem; we learn because something has caused us to want to know. But school has no natural motivation associated with it. Students go there because they have no choice. The same is true of most training situations.[17]

When the ultimate learn-as-you-go opportunity crashed onto American shores—a global pandemic—all presidential efforts to remedy the effects of such an unknown and unprecedented event were on the table. When Trump considered any and all possibly relevant remedies, he was being pragmatic. His goal was to solve this problem. Were hydroxychloroquine and ivermectin effective therapies? Were vaccines, complete shutdowns and masking of the masses helpful? The reality, however, of a media hostile to the sitting president threw a wrench into what ordinarily would have been a scientifically and medically legitimate work in progress. As it was, lies and censorship trumped science and the American public struggled and suffered under the results.

It's all about being teachable, as well as paying it forward. Visualization is also an ingredient to being a successful man or woman, at least in Trump's eyes. Have a purpose in what you are doing, and see it through to the end, picturing the project before you get to work on it. "So I want you to ask yourself: what is it that you are aiming for?" Trump writes in *Think Like a Champion.*

> What precisely is your motivation? What's the point of building a bridge if you're not sure you want to get to the other side, or if you don't know what you'll do once you get there? A bridge must serve a specific purpose, and your goals have to be just that specific. Visualization is a powerful tool for bringing your intentions into focus. [18]

Trump advises success seekers to also study something other than basic business—he points to English literature, more specifically the work of William Shakespeare:

> I was having a conversation a few years ago with a few people when one guy mentioned that the Trump name had become a famous brand around the world and then added, "What's in a name?" he then sort of laughed and said to me, "In your case, a lot!" I noticed that one guy seemed out of the loop about the quip. So I said, "That's Shakespeare. 'What's in a name' is a famous line from Shakespeare." So he still looked perplexed and asked, "From what?" And although I knew it was from Romeo and Juliet, I said, "Look it up. You might learn some interesting things along the way"... Don't be left out! Take a few hours a week to review the classics in literature or history or something outside of your usual range of interests. Limiting yourself is not the best choice.[19]

Trump also calls on Shakespeare in giving some of his best career advice.

> Shakespeare put it this way, in a famous quote from Julius Caesar: "The fault is not in our stars, dear Brutus, but in ourselves." That's a clear message. We are responsible for ourselves. We are responsible for our own luck. What an empowering thought! If you see responsibility as a bum deal, then you are not seeing it for what it really is—a great opportunity... What will separate you from the complaining crowd will be how you choose to look at your situation. If you believe you are in control of it—and you are—you will know exactly who to look for when you need help: yourself.[20]

Trump uses the words *tenacious* and *indomitable* to pinpoint his keys to success, which, in his case, has often meant facing a firewall of cynics and critics, such as when he moved his operations into Manhattan despite being told that this was a bad time to be investing in real estate in the Big Apple. "I overcame some great setbacks just by being obstinate. I refused to give in or give up. To me, that's an integrity of purpose that cannot be defeated or interfered with to any significant level. Being steadfast in your intentions can reap great results."[21]

But Donald Trump had a village too when it came to acquiring those high-rise properties he sought in Manhattan real-estate. Aside from the boost he might have received initially from building with his father, he was a natural at drawing those people he needed to help him to rise. He had a knack for enticing potential business partners with convincing hyperbole such as "It's the greatest project," or bankers and city officials with "It's the most spectacular view you'll ever see." Call it chutzpah, call it energy, call it "hot to trot" (according to Jordan Gruzen, an architect on one of Donald's early projects).[22] Whatever you call it, Trump had it in spades. And he used it to bring not only attention but also influence and power into his corner of the ring.

Ned Eichler, Trump's real-estate associate on the ambitious West Side Rail Yards development, was "taken by the sheer energy on the other end of the [phone] line" when he first spoke with the yet-unknown Manhattan developer (still just a twenty-something dreamer).[23] Writes Gwenda Blair in *The Trumps*. "That air of confidence" and "his overwhelming eagerness [were] engaging."[24] Also, it was an "intense drive... that made up for his lack of cash."[25] This same chutzpah (which, by the way, is Yiddish for *audacity, nerve*—guts, if you will) became The Donald's hallmark for drawing people to him—like bees to honey. If it wasn't deal-makers and takers, it was New York City elites, social movers, and shakers, and a constant buzz of an obsessive press, including society-page reporters and tabloid gossip columnists. But later it became The Apprentice wannabes, celebrities of all makes and models, golf aficionados, and only lately an American public swarming to his rallies to cheer and chant for a man they helped install in the White House.

A relentlessly positive mindset helps, too. Trump hit what might have been the lowest point in his business career around 1990, when he found himself about a billion dollars in debt with banks threatening foreclosure. This was just after Trump had indulged in a third casino, an airline, the world's second-largest yacht, and the Plaza Hotel. Painted into a corner with seemingly no way out, Trump engaged in weeks of 24/7 negotiations, coming out of them relatively unscathed, and still very much in business. In a 2009 interview with *Psychology Today*, he gave credit to Norman Vincent Peale's all-time bestselling book *The Power of Positive Thinking*, giving a shout-out to his father Fred's friendship with Peale while calling himself a "firm believer in the power of being positive." He added, "What helped is I refused to give in to the negative circumstances and never lost faith in myself. I didn't believe I was finished even when the newspapers were saying so."[26]

Even then, "fake news" wasn't going to stop Trump.

Chapter Eight
Master of the Mic

"It is very common in this country to find great facility of expression and less common to find great lucidity of thought. The combination of the two in one person is very uncommon; but whenever you do find it, you have a great man."

-Lincoln's remark to British journalist Edward Dicey, c. 1862-1863

WITHOUT A DOUBT, DONALD TRUMP PROVED A MASTER OF THE POLITICAL stage, building a unique crowd-pleasing public image and donning a style of speaking that clearly and simply roused crowds of eager fans. A head-on, in-your-face kind of boldness guided this provocative virtuoso of the American soap box.

Trump didn't just master the art of public speaking, he turned it onto its listeners' ear, treating it as performance art. He did it in manners unique to his well-cultivated persona with style captivating audiences with plain, impactful language that resonated, trumpeted authenticity, stirred emotions, and titillated followers—all rarely with the benefit of a teleprompter. Trump is an original—*maverick* might be a better word—speaking, and writing, with a style, clarity, power, and panache unlike any other major politician of the day. When this man addressed the masses, people didn't just listen (or read), they bought in 100 percent, hearing and seeing verbiage that rarely needed a dictionary to be understood. Master communicator; the best of the best.

It chafes the back sides of Trump's detractors to no end that he can fill speaking venues with enthusiastic audiences that hang on his every word. More often than not, what Trump says reflects exactly what his followers are thinking, and he does it with a certain amount of performance art— something he readily admits. "A great portion of life and business involved acting," Trump says in Think Like a Champion.

Life is a performance art, no matter what field you are in. I've come to understand that fact over the years, and it's a helpful thing to realize. It includes people skills, negotiation skills, public relations, salesmanship, and the ability to read your audience, whether that audience is four people in your office or forty thousand at a speech. The same technique applies.[1]

It's helpful to note that *Think Like a Champion* was published in 2010, meaning Trump wrote those words about five years before he frisbeed his hat into the ring for the 2016 presidential election. Political handlers didn't teach that stuff to Trump; more than likely he taught them about injecting panache into politics.

Trump developed the ability to entertain early in his life via his mastery of bigger and better showmanship. He used savvy self-promotion to build his brand—in large part through his popular reality TV show *The Apprentice*. In terms of getting his message across, his methods worked wonders as a populist president. A performer's craft is honed through ample preparation. Getting up on stage, getting behind a podium, or standing in front of a live camera and mic as a crowd presses in around you, is not the time to start thinking about what you're going to say or how you're going to say it, how you're going to use your hands, or when and how you want to change your voice's inflection. Whatever entertainment value Trump brings to a public setting is built on years of practice and constant fine-tuning. He isn't just winging it up there.

Trump has said,

I also thought about the people who would be in the audience instead of my own performance. That perspective frees you up from nervousness to allow you to focus on and know your audience . . . You also have to have the goods to hold your audience, no matter what the size may be. Performers prepare for every performance. That's showmanship, and that's life. Prepare yourself every day. Learn, know, and show. It's a proven formula . . .[2]

Trump showcased his winning formula for performance success—and communicative success—by keeping his show *The Apprentice* going strong for fourteen seasons, pulling in high ratings much of the time it was on the air. His preferred audience was the general public; his media philosophy is that there is no such thing as "bad" publicity, and through his shameless bravado and accompanying hype he has always kept the press—even those in the practice of cranking out "fake news"—and the public always wanting more. "I play to people's fantasies," Trump wrote in 1987, thirty years before he was sworn in as the nation's forty-fifth president. "People may not always think big themselves, but they can still get very excited by those who do. That's why a little hyperbole never hurts. People want to believe that something is the biggest and the greatest and the most spectacular." [3]

If we can go back in time even another decade-plus, to 1976, we can see thirty-year-old Donald Trump featured in *The New York Times*, expounding on the millions he had already made in metropolitan real estate and showing off his penthouse apartment and Cadillac. As part of providing background for the high-profile story, Trump allowed the reporter to accompany him as he visited job sites and tag along for lunches at the "21" club before taking an evening flight to the West Coast for another round of deal making.

"Young and ambitious, Trump worked just as hard at building the image as he did at expanding his real estate empire," *Associated Press* reporter Nancy Benac wrote in 2016. "Along the way, he honed the communications skills that would benefit him at the negotiating table, turn him into a reality TV star, and launch a presidential campaign."[4]

Trump inherited much of his drive from his businessman dad Fred—at least his penchant for shrewd promotion. At times their promotions pushed the line of good taste (of course, the definition of which depends heavily on your perspective and perhaps even your faith). Fred Trump—and keep in mind this goes well back in terms of decades—spent a good chunk of his life constructing homes and apartments in Brooklyn and Queens, where he used various promotional gimmicks to push his product at would-be buyers, and there were many. One of Fast Fred's gimmicks was filling a bulldozer bucket with beautiful, bikini-clad women. Other times, Fred released balloons stuffed with fifty-dollar coupons over a beach full of Coney Island sunbathers. Often, the lobbies of his apartment buildings included bird cages that had been positioned to catch the eyes (and ears) of passersby.

"(Donald is) a media natural," said Aaron Kall, director of the University of Michigan's Debate Institute and the school's debate team, comparing the younger Trump's ability to perform as being on the level of "a maestro... He really understands audiences and tailors a message to what he thinks that they want to hear."[5]

What Trump's detractors and naysayers don't seem to grasp is that the scathing comments he makes in press conferences that seem off the cuff and reckless—or his highly opinionated tweets, sometimes several a day—are just part of his work as an experienced and modern-day, plugged-in communicator who knows how to market himself. He's been doing it going on fifty years, beginning right out of college.

Benac writes:

> Long before NBC's The Apprentice turned Trump into a reality TV star in 2004 [more than twenty years ago! This guy is no unwitting novice], he was advancing his biz-whiz image in TV and movie cameos, chatting up Howard Stern on the radio and filming ads for Pizza Hut, McDonald's, and more. Then, over fourteen seasons of The Apprentice and Celebrity Apprentice, he sharpened his ability to work the camera, think on his feet, and promote the Trump brand.
>
> As a presidential candidate, he's drawn on those same skills to keep himself in the news, dishing out provocations and insults sure to guarantee the public's attention.[6]

Many big shots, like those in the business world, grow obsessively protective of their millions/billions, striving to shun the press and keep out of the public eye. Not Donald Trump. As the subject of overwrought media coverage for well over half his life, he has willingly subjected himself to the constant attention. Along the way he had learned as much about how the media game is played as those in the news and entertainment business have learned about him. Trump can bathe as comfortably in the hot waters of intense media coverage as he can dish it back at those looking to pin him to the mat. A message to any newshound planning to go in for the kill? Wouldn't be prudent.

Trump can't stay out of the news, nor does he want to. Good news is okay by him; bad news is, too. Fake news gives him something to crow about; it feeds into his nonstop narrative of self above circumstances. No news means it's time for him to make something happen. Media attacks on him only make him stronger. When the story broke in 1990 that he was having an affair with Marla Maples, Trump spent eight straight days on the cover of the *New York Post*—New York's tabloid version of the *National Enquirer*. Such coverage—literally, on the cover—just didn't happen in those days. What would be a nightmare even for a public-relations whiz and master of spin was catnip to Trump. He craved the attention, and yet he was as much admired by the public as he was scorned in other quarters. This is a big part of how he communicates, and his staunchest following is the general public—average Joes and Janes.

Susan Mulcahy, a New York writer, editor, and consultant, and former tabloid writer, wrote a piece for politico.com in 2016 (before Trump had won the Republican presidential nomination) that painted a picture of how even the tabloids' best arrows just bounce off him, like Superman in a hail of bullets, dating back to the 1980s:

> If you worked for a newspaper in New York in the 1980s, you had to write about Trump. As editor of the New York Post's Page Six, and later as a columnist for New York Newsday, I needed to fill a lot of space, ideally with juicy stories of the rich and powerful, and Trump more than obliged. I wrote about his real estate deals. I wrote about his wife, his yacht, his parties, his houses. At times, I would let several months go by without a single column mention of The Donald; this doubtless upset him, as he loves Page Six and used to have it brought to him the moment it arrived in his office. But eventually I returned to the subject, as did a legion of other writers. We didn't see it at the time, but item by inky item we were turning him into a New York icon.[7]

Trump is an original. Anyone who has paid any attention to him over the years knows this to be true. Think about it. Name anyone in American political history who can compare to Trump. For one thing, as his son Donald Jr. says, "There's no one else like him," starting with the fact that his father doesn't believe in political correctness "where every statement you make, you have to vet very carefully through thousands of people. But if people really break down what he's trying to say, there's no malice in there. He's just cutting through the nonsense and getting to the point and not wasting time . . . He's an amazing guy, and I wouldn't change a thing about him. He really is a unique individual."[8]

He's unique in other ways as well, such as his resilience. A cloak of Teflon always seems to adorn the Donald, protecting him from crises and controversies that would cripple the reputations and lofty political aspirations of other prominent people. Instead, these slide off Trump, like raindrops off a tin roof.

"The rules that govern others just don't apply to Trump," writes Jackie Calmes, at the time a Los Angeles Times reporter, noting that Trump the businessman's willingness to carry hundreds of millions of dollars of debts on his books and file multiple bankruptcies for his company's casinos have failed to slow down the juggernaut that is Donald Trump, the Trump organization, and, now, his breadth of acquired political capital. "Even in 2004," Calmes writes, "as Trump's casino business was in bankruptcy again, *The New York Times* notes—in words that would ring true during his campaign years later—'His name has become such a byword for success that even the most humiliating reverses barely dent his reputation.'"[9]

Of course, this hasn't kept the press from trying. For instance, there was that time in January 2017 when a report filed by a *Time* magazine reporter went viral. The reporter claimed Trump had removed a bust of Dr. Martin Luther King Jr. from a White House office and replaced it with a bust of Winston Churchill, apparently suggesting on his first day in office that Trump was a "white, imperialistic, racist" president, and now America was stuck with him. This being Inauguration Day 2017, much of the national media swooped in and picked up the story in what would infamously become the first instance of "fake news" in the Trump presidency.

The *Time* report was proven false before the day was out. The King bust had been there all along, hidden from the view of the reporter who had failed to be diligent in verifying the bust's location. "Keep in mind, all this reporting happened immediately after Trump had given an inaugural speech that was completely antidiscriminatory and reaffirmed Trump's position that to be racist is to be unpatriotic and unAmerican," former U.S. Speaker of the House Newt Gingrich writes in *Understanding Trump*.[10] A part of the segment of Trump's inaugural address that Gingrich cites in his book follows:

> It is time to remember that old wisdom our soldiers will never forget: that whether we are black or brown or white, we all bleed the same red blood of patriots, we all enjoy the same glorious freedoms, and we all salute the same great American flag.

> And whether a child is born in the urban sprawl of Detroit or the windswept plains of Nebraska, they look up at the same night sky, they fill their heart with the same dreams, and they are infused with the breath of life by the same almighty Creator."

Finally, Gingrich adds, "But these words—which came out of the president's mouth in front of the entire nation—did not fit the media's narrative of who this president is, so they ignored him."[11]

An argument could be made that Trump is a master public speaker. But perhaps a better way of describing him—and now we get into semantics—is that he masters speaking *to the public*. Trump just doesn't fit the mold of classic master public speaker with perfectly trained lilt and carefully cultivated posture and bearing; his style is a marked departure from other skilled orators. Yet his ability to be easily and thoroughly understood, and consistently embraced, by rapt audiences is unquestioned. Trump is rough around the edges, and that makes him unique in his own appealing manner. He is not what you'd call a smooth talker, but smooth might be better left for radio deejays, as he is certainly effective in his own way.

In today's world of nonstop news and entertainment, with an emphasis on the latter growing stronger by the day, there is no keeping news out of the media. That's because whenever there is a lack of worthy news on a given day, media members can fill the gaps with their own narrative. This has been going on for years, and it continues to ramp up. The news need not be supported by facts or objective truths in a world where opinion, conjecture, bias, and political correctness provide ample content. Often this content resembles nothing but a lot of noise, and it's where those who most ardently tout concepts such as "diversity" and "inclusion" practice hate speech.

Contemporary media doesn't need statements issued by the White House press office or through press briefings to report on the presidency; they can say whatever they want when they want. They will constantly drum up their own narrative to whatever tempo of drumbeat they choose to use at any given time. If President Trump or candidate Trump were to keep silent or speak daily with access given to the media, it makes no difference—he exercises free rein. But with Trump, the media can do very little to stop him from getting his unfiltered message out to the people. His words are untainted by media and other critics, and he accomplished this almost every day he was in office. His main *modus operandi* in going to the people was through his frequent use of Twitter and later Truth Social, as well as his many public appearances around the United States and throughout the world. He knows the national media can't resist chasing him and covering him. At times, he even shifted the media narrative through his determined influence or by simply baiting the press, calling them out for their own mistakes and biased reporting. He could pin them down when they pushed a part of their narrative that he described as "fake news." The media dishes it at him relentlessly, and he dishes it right back.

Again, this tactic goes back to the Trump maxim that while good publicity is preferable to bad, bad publicity—from a bottom-line perspective—is occasionally preferable to no publicity at all. Trump knows that controversy sells, period. He says whatever he wants to say, and taking that chutzpah into the political world has tipped a lot of cows along the way. Trump is amazingly effective and comfortable when it comes to speaking extemporaneously. Time and again, such as when he was on the campaign trail in 2016, 2020, and again in 2024, Trump frequently spoke without notes or a teleprompter or, apparently, without much preparation at all. This approach would have horrified his walk-on-eggshells predecessor Barack Obama and his most recent political opponent Joe Biden. Actually, Biden has gone off script hundreds of cringe-worthy times during his half century in politics, straying into misspeaking purgatory and staying there long enough to remind the world that some very offensive things are truly better left unsaid.

It is the performance art aspect of public communication that Trump seems to enjoy the most, noting that, "A great portion of life and business involves acting," as Trump writes in *Think Like a Champion.*

> Most of us have been exposed to the work of Shakespeare, and he spends a great deal of time dwelling on the characteristics of human nature. Some of the examples are extreme, but they aren't so far-fetched as to be unbelievable, or Shakespeare wouldn't still be performed today. There's something about his work that is timeless, and the timeliness comes from his insight into human nature...

> I think most people want to be the best they can be. That's probably one reason you're reading this right now—you've chosen the high road, the path to more knowledge and experience. It's one of the reasons I enjoy giving speeches and teaching. [12]

As much as Trump might enjoy public speaking, experts in the craft fault him for what has been described as his "juvenile" vocabulary, jumbled syntax, casualness when it comes to accuracy, his demeaning tone, his weakness on policy details, and a voice characterized as thin and nasally. Picky, picky.

Ruth Sherman, a public-speaking coach quoted by Benac in her "Road to Debate" piece, referenced earlier in this chapter, suggests that while Trump, in her expert opinion, has a poor speaking voice, much of the American public has heard him so much for so long (that's what fourteen seasons of *The Apprentice* on TV can do for you) that they are willing to give him "a pass" on his speaking voice.

"He doesn't get criticized for the quality of his speaking voice, but he should," Sherman says. "It's a thin voice. It's not smooth. It's somewhat nasal."[13]

Nonetheless, Trump has an ability to draw large crowds wherever he goes to speak, crowds of people who come on their own volition. They didn't need to be bused in by event organizers looking to manufacture a full house so there would be no—or at least just a few—empty seats in the direction of where the cameras were pointed.

With Trump, his public speaking engagements take on the airs and ambiance of tent revivals, without the religious trimmings, yet with a spirit of secular salvation that few politicians have ever been able to generate. The enthusiasm of his listeners isn't just palpable, it is genuine, with audience members willing to lend their hearts as well as their ears to the spoken message. And it's been done without teleprompters, because he doesn't need that crutch to find the words to speak from the heart and soul to tell people what they want, and need, to hear. His is the power of positive thinking, the entrepreneurial mindset. Trump focuses on what can be achieved with personal work ethic and responsibility. It's great news for the people and bad news for political opponents.

"You know, I don't believe in teleprompters," Trump has said.

You read a speech, and you read it—and then you leave, and nobody goes crazy. I give it very much from the heart. You know, the greatest speaker I think I've ever witnessed was Dr. Norman Vincent Peale, and he would speak the power of positive thinking. He would speak so much—and he'd bring it into modern-day life. He talked about success stories and people that were successful and became alcoholics, and then they conquered it... I grew up watching that. He wasn't reading. I've [heard] plenty of pastors and ministers that read. It's not the same thing.

You go into Mobile with thirty-one thousand or Dallas with twenty thousand people—and you don't even have literally notes in front of you. It's a little bit nerve-wracking because you know, maybe who knows, right? But it's exciting, and the energy really does something to me that's incredible. You saw the crowds, you saw the response to standing ovations for five and ten minutes sometimes, so it's very exciting. [14]

It's no mistake or coincidence that Trump speeches generate the fervor of a religious revival. As mentioned in this book, Trump periodically sought out the counsel and eventual friendships of a number of Christian leaders, pastors, and evangelists, even before he ran for president. Some came to him. At first most were skeptical of Trump, questioning his sincerity and where he stood with the Christian faith. Eventually many opened up to Trump on the practice of reaching out to people and spreading the good word, even if, in his case, it wasn't often taken straight from scripture.

One of those Trump "converts" was Dallas evangelist Lance Wallnau, a conservative Pentecostal Christian, who, in September 2015, found himself going to New York to join other Christian leaders to meet with Trump at Trump Tower. Wallnau enjoyed his congregating with other like-minded Christian leaders and the chance to meet the presidential candidate, but upon boarding the airplane for the flight back to Dallas, he knew he still wasn't sold on Trump. Then something happened.

"The Word of the Lord . . . about the Presidential candidate—it came to me. This was new territory for me," Wallnau said, "but I came home, and when I was standing in my study in my office, I heard these words: 'Donald Trump is a wrecking ball to the spirit of political correctness'. . . And that was the moment that I got behind Donald Trump. I was enthusiastic for him from that moment on."[15] At one point during Trump's meeting with the Christian leaders, some black as well as white, the conversation turned to what should happen during a worship service when the preacher is preaching a good sermon and someone in the audience feels inspired to storm the pulpit and attempt to grab the microphone away from the preacher. How would you deal with that?

"Nobody even stopped to say, 'Let's be careful how we answer this,'" Wallnau said,

> Because in an African-American church, the very thought of you getting up and interrupting the man—no, they've got more respect for the man of God, like the Catholic respects the priest. In the African-American church, you'd better respect clergy. They told

Trump, "We'd take the person out—and we may not even be pleasant on the way out the door. We wouldn't be worried about hurting your feelings if you're going to try to storm the pulpit when the preacher's preaching."

According to Wallnau, Trump waited until the other men in the room were finished speaking, then looked them in the eye and said, "That's all I'm saying. The rallies are like my church service. I'm the preacher, and I'm trying to deliver my sermon."[16]

Trump's campaign rallies were and are the stuff of legend and continued to draw enthusiastic crowds of eager fans into the next decade. In a 2019 podcast, *Wall Street Journal* reporter Mike Bender described a Trump rally as a multi-day event for many Trump supporters. They would hear about the event a week or two in advance, and soon the line would start forming at the venue. Aspiring attendees would arrive early to increase their chances of getting a seat before the fire marshal closed down further admittance into the venue.

According to Bender:

There is an old-time tent revival aspect to these rallies. And a sort of ritual of it. And there's a certain validation to it, too. I mean, for a lot of Trump supporters, and especially the Front Row Joes, they were among the first people in America to recognize the resonance of Trump's political message. And they were right. They picked a horse early on, stuck by him, and they won.

All of the people I talked to, the one thing they talk about is the energy they get from these rallies, and it's kind of psychic cleansing that comes from ninety minutes of participating in the same chants and cheering the same applause lines as twenty thousand other people, like-minded people, that a lot of them don't get out of their normal daily lives.[17]

Still, the attacks keep coming in Trump's direction. Though touted by media as legit journalism, these are in fact a transparent veil for liberal thought and culture, and even strands of Marxist activists, to bring down Trump. Through it all, he absorbs the punches and keeps on ticking . . . and thriving.

"I don't mind being attacked," Trump says.

I use the media the way the media uses me—to attract attention. Once I have that attention, it's up to me to use it to my advantage. I learned a long time ago that if you're not afraid to be outspoken, the media will write about you or beg you to come on their shows . . . So sometimes I make outrageous comments and give them what they want—viewers and readers—in order to make a point . . . But now I am using those talents, honed through years of tremendous success, to inspire people to think that our country can get better and be great again and that we can turn things around. [18]

Donald Trump's ability to fill arenas with capacity crowds cements him as a popular speaker, but Trump is not known as a literary virtuoso, a man of letters. He's more a man of characters, as in how many characters can you squeeze into one tweet or post and hope to get your message out to American citizens across the country? Through the first three and a half years of his presidency, Trump had sent out untold thousands of tweets, many of them crossing the lines of political correctness, but all of them with a purpose in mind—to reveal to Americans what is on his mind without being filtered by media. Trump's use of social media, particularly Twitter and later Truth Social, has pushed him over the top in terms of U.S. presidents making effective use of personal communication ability and tools at their disposal.

"President Trump has already proven to be an expert in using social media to bypass the elite news media and speak directly with the American people through Facebook, Twitter, YouTube, or other new social media platforms," Gingrich writes in *Trump's America*. "He could use these skills to connect directly with the American people—much like FDR did with his fireside chats, a series of radio broadcasts he made during his presidency." [19]

Trump has often been known to take control of the day's news cycle soon after he gets out of bed by posting out to millions of his supporters whatever happens to be on his mind. It might be a tweet about a possible executive order he has been contemplating, or a critical comment about a political opponent such as Joe Biden, taking to task a Democratic mayor of a city unwilling to curtail protest-related violence in his or her city, or calling out the corruption in the DC swamp or Deep State political bullies. No topic was off-limits and Donald Trump makes his own rules for what is acceptable.

"It was routine for Trump to get millions of dollars' worth of free media without spending a penny," Gingrich points out in *Understanding Trump*.[20]

If all else fails, in today's world anyway, there's always Trump to dish it right. There's this exchange between Trump and pollster/pundit Frank Luntz during a televised one-on-one Q&A in 2016 in which Luntz opens by tossing Trump a softball question about public education policy. Trump swings and connects:

> "Common Core has to be ended, It's a disaster," Trump said, earning applause by echoing every other GOP candidate's answer on the subject. But then he added Trumpian color: "It is a way of taking care of the people in Washington that frankly, I don't even think they give a damn about education, half of them. I am sure some maybe do."
>
> "Do you want to use that word in this forum?" Luntz asked with a smile. The audience leaned in.
>
> "I will, I will. Because people want to hear the truth, Frank," Trump said. "I watch you all the time; they want to hear the truth."
>
> Applause erupted.
>
> "I mean, exactly what Frank said is what is wrong with our country. We are so politically correct that we cannot move anymore."[21]

Donald Trump was notorious for ad-libbing and going off-script during his rally speeches. Audiences knew when he followed the teleprompter and when he added his own sideline quips, thoughts, and hyperbole that only Trump could pepper throughout an otherwise carefully written speech, and they loved it! In between memorized sound bites the inevitable colorful language, stream of consciousness comments and personal Trumpisms fed the crowds during his presidential campaigns. No one knew what he was going to say next. Even as president, Trump maintained a mostly unfiltered pathway from mind to mouth. And not likely to change . . . ever.

At one August 2016 Campaign rally in Michigan, he implored African Americans for their vote with "What have you got to lose?" He repeated the plea several times before finalizing it with an ad-lib expletive undoubtedly generated by thousands of excited rally-goers—"What the hell do you have to lose?!"

Call it the "fire & brimstone" from a pulpit only Trump could fill.

Chapter Nine
Take the Lead

"I confess that I desire to be re-elected. God knows I do not want the labor and responsibility of the office for another four years. But I have the common pride of humanity to wish my past four years Administration endorsed."

-Abraham Lincoln remark, c. 1864

THE LEADERSHIP DEBATE CONTINUES AND MIGHT NEVER END: ARE GREAT leaders born or made? Is it nature or is it nurture that imbues a young Donald Trump with the right ingredients to handle the reins of an entity as considerable and consequential as America? On closer look, it took both nature and nurture to provide the ingredients necessary for influencing the making of the political and presidential phenomenon that is Trump.

The seeds of presidential-style leadership are planted in childhood, when parental upbringing and influence can give (or deny) a child the foundation he or she needs to have sufficient firm footing to handle the reins, rigors, and risks of leadership as they grow into such roles. Studies of prominent, successful leaders have shown that many came from households in which parents were authoritative while also giving their child the slack to make their own choices. Such parents also support their child and offer encouragement and compliments when earned, but without spoiling the child and giving them a sense of entitlement. They also let their children take chances and experience the consequences of them—even the ones resulting from bad choices, allowing the child to understand risk and results without the parent(s) rescuing them at the last minute.[1]

A happy childhood, or at least the impression of having had one, can be related to the sense of self and social connectedness that contributes to leadership and healthy adult behaviors.[2] Trump had a relatively happy childhood (at least until age thirteen, when he was enrolled in a military school to smooth off the rough edges.) And a nurturing and secure home life contributes to that sense of happiness during those impressionable childhood years. In fact, the family dynamic is one of the most important determiners of budding leadership—stability matters.[3]

Donald Trump grew up in a stable family, one that offered love and security, and at least a modicum of nurture mixed with discipline. Profanity was forbidden in the Trump household, where there were curfews and plenty of other rules that set firm boundaries for the five children. With all the house rules came ample discipline, with mom Mary giving the dad, Fred, a daily report when he got back from work at the end of the day. The daily report card provided details on who acted up and who would be punished, which often came at the big end of a wooden spoon.

"My family is very important to me and always has been," a grown-up Trump declared decades later, referring not only to his own family but the one he grew up in back in Jamaica Estates, New York. "I'm happiest when I'm with them."[4]

Born in 1946, Donnie Trump was at the forefront of the baby boom generation, grouping together those born during the period 1946 through 1964, with that first wave arriving in the wake of the end of the Second World War. This generation had a dynamic all its own, one that undoubtedly shaped young Donald Trump for life, as author Gwenda Blair explains in her book *The Trumps:*

> Although this generation's primary identity would be as members of their own families, they would also develop a secondary role as members of the baby boom family. Together with their boomer sisters and brothers, they would grow up on television, rock and roll, and the cold war. But for those born, as Donald Trump was, at the beginning of the boom, there may have been something more. Because the war had interrupted normal patterns of marriage and childbearing, children born in the first few years of the baby boom included a higher-than-normal proportion of firstborns. In turn, instead of having the full range of personality attributes associated with children of a variety of birth orders, children in the first wave of the baby boom would tend to have a similar, firstborn character: assertive, ambitious, and, above all, successful. Further, because of this heavily firstborn environment, a kind of herd effect may have taken over, with playmates and classmates who were not firstborns acting as if they were . . . Donald Trump was one of these faux

firstborns. Although the fourth-born in his family, by all accounts he was self-assured, determined, and positive from the start. [5]

With the war over and the world again safe from the likes of Adolph Hitler, the Third Reich, and other like-minded tyrants, America hit the ground running. Soldiers around the world were returning home, new cars were rolling off the assembly lines in Detroit, and the first models of television sets were being planted in almost every living room or den in the United States.

It was a time in America, one that would last into the early sixties, when few people worried about locking their doors. It was also a time when kids freely roamed from one friend's house to another in the neighborhood; this was a world in which everyone knew their neighbor. Even the well-monitored (if not always well-mannered) Trump kids were also free to go next door or across the street to see and play with friends. There were always other possibilities beyond just the four walls of your own house.

For the Trump kids, their favorite go-to neighbor was Bernice Able MacIntosh and Bernice's daughter, Heather. Bernice could also speak German and years earlier had been friends with Fred Trump's mother. "It seemed like every morning I would have two or three Trumps at the breakfast table with Heather," Bernice said many years later. "There were three cookie jars, and they were always open. So was the refrigerator. The Trumps didn't have that [freedom] at their house, so they came over to mine."[6]

The Trump kids were close to Bernice and Heather, enough so that Mrs. MacIntosh would buy gifts for them. Donald's favorites were toy vehicles. "Every Christmas and for each birthday, I'd buy him the strongest truck I could find," Bernice said. "He'd always take it apart immediately. By the time my daughter got home from his birthday party, he'd have dismantled it. 'Oh, Mom, he's got it all in pieces,' she'd say."[7]

Trump also had the benefit of specialized schooling from the time he was three years old, beginning with the Carousel Pre-School, which was the nursery program nearby in Jamaica Estates, which emphasized hands-on learning experiences, of which building blocks no doubt became one of young Donald's greatest early influences and passions.[8]

Writing in his bestselling book *The Art of the Deal*, Trump saw himself as a natural leader from an early age, saying,

I was always something of a leader in my neighborhood. Much the way it is today, people either liked me a lot, or they didn't like me at all. In my own crowd I was very well-liked, and I tended to be the kid that others followed. As an adolescent, I was mostly interested in creating mischief, because for some reason I liked to stir things up, and I liked to test people.[9]

Donald Trump was the poster boy for the power of positive thinking, a key recipe ingredient for making and being a strong leader. In order to inspire and motivate others, a leader must have an optimistic approach to life and an upbeat spirit in order to fend off or at least bounce back quickly from verbal attacks. Trump was on the receiving end of plenty of them.

If Trump ever has pause or remorse for anything he has ever said or done, he rarely, if ever, shows or speaks it. His outsized personality is about staying bold and pushing ahead, leading from the front, such as he did in October 2020, when he joined millions of other Americans who had contracted the Covid-19 coronavirus. The infection knocked Trump down for a few days, sending him to the hospital for personalized 24/7 care, but thanks to his strength of will and body as well and the expert care provided by a team of physicians, he was on his feet and back in the White House within three days and soon after back out on the presidential campaign trail, as vigorous and outspoken as ever.

Leadership usually isn't a great career choice for wallflowers, shrinking violets, and anyone who is afraid to speak up and be counted, even when everything inside of them is screaming to speak up and make a stand— even if it means being perceived as rude at times. Donald Trump is the first to admit that he can be "self-assertive in a rude, noisy or overbearing way"—the very definition of brash.

"I don't mind being called brash because to me it's being bold, it's having energy, it's getting things done," Trump said some years ago, recalling a *Newsweek* magazine ad from the eighties that included a photograph of him with the caption, "Few things in life are as brash as *Newsweek*," added Trump, he of the thick skin: "But the constraints are to be considered, and my momentum is carefully monitored. I'm not exactly brash in that sense, but I know you can't get things done if you're too timid. My persona will never be one of the wallflower—I'd rather build walls than cling to them."[10]

"You can't be scared. You do your thing, you hold your ground, you stand up tall, and whatever happens, happens." [11]

Like him or detest him, anyone who has seen and/or heard Trump speak—either in front of huge crowds at campaign rallies or in a room one-on-one with either a world leader or an inquiring reporter— can't dispute his unbridled confidence. He aims high and believes strongly in the acquisition of practical knowledge. In his case that has often meant being a leader who uses his hands and doesn't mind getting them dirty, either literally or proverbially.

"[Trump] believes in aiming high and accomplishing what others say is impossible," political ally Newt Gingrich writes in *Understanding Trump*.

> Trump values people who have gained practical knowledge—knowledge that must be learned by doing rather than by hearing a lecture or reading a book. Trump himself learned the bulk of the real estate trade by working with his father—not while he was attending the University of Pennsylvania's Wharton School.[12]

* * *

A capable, competent leader has a strong moral core and code, and Donald Trump can boil his down to a simple question: is this the right thing to do? And is it just? Trump's pride in a strong America and its Judeo-Christian underpinnings is a large part of this moral core. The decade in which Donald was between five and thirteen years old can be described as a "John Wayne America" —the America of the 1950s. It was a time in his life in which he undoubtedly experienced John Wayne—and his big screen hero masculinity—in movies like *Rio Bravo* or *The High and the Mighty,* movies in which the good guys and bad guys were easy to discern. Brody and Lamb explain in *The Faith of Donald J. Trump*:

> The "John Wayne America" ideal man sits tall in the saddle; doesn't whine or complain; fights and dies for things that matter; exhibits courage in the face of danger; works hard—maybe even an unbalanced amount; provides for his family; builds things (institutions, buildings, businesses) that others inhabit; leaves the world a better place; may speak with machismo—but never effeminacy; and communicates hope even when it defies logic.[13]

A black and white world of right and wrong plays strongly into Trump's belief system, and though he himself isn't always good, he maintains a moral code that understands the clear boundaries of good and evil. In the

1950s Americans believed that the communists were evil and America was the force for good in the world. Later, President Reagan would put a lasting label of "Evil Empire" on the Soviet Union.

A cursory check of Donald Trump's fascinating past doesn't reveal any great physical feats worthy of the Olympics, but tales of what has been described as his "Olympic vigor" became more common following his election as president in November 2016. And since physical, mental, emotional endurance are a leadership requirement, Trump used his for surviving and even thriving in the endless haranguing he endured as both candidate and president.

For years after his 2016 election, Trump was continuously under assault by devious political opponents and an outrageously biased media working in tandem to destroy his presidential and political careers with conspiracies ranging from the ultimately false charges of Russian collusion and election interference to a three-ring impeachment circus followed by endless lawfare and fake indictments meant to knock him flat.

Not only did Trump prove himself a fighter worthy of the U.S. presidency and leader of the Republican Party, but also a highly skilled politician (even though he refused to call himself one.) And, although raised in wealth, Donald Trump acquired appreciation for sweat equity earlier in life—back when he was slinging newspapers onto doorsteps and picking up nails at job sites—that prepared him for leadership positions over time. "His work ethic is actually hard to describe," said Mike Pence, Trump's first vice president.

> I heard once that President Teddy Roosevelt was described by a contemporary as pure energy, and I've often said that must come around every hundred years at the White House, because the President and I will generally talk early, we'll talk late, we talk throughout the day. It's amazing... He has an indefatigable capacity. Every day is a new day; we're back working on what we came here to do. I ultimately believe that springs from his faith and his upbringing, and a lifetime of building and overcoming. When you're president, there is a need to balance two important concepts: law and grace.[14]

While Trump's indefatigability and world-class fighting spirit has come as a shock to his liberal Democratic opponents, it doesn't surprise him at all. Trump has long fancied himself an elite athlete, although it's hard to tell if he is being facetious at times, such as when he once declared that he was definitely "the best baseball player in New York," claiming that he might have turned pro had the pay been better. Although Trump certainly exaggerated his athletic skills and potential for major-league success on a baseball diamond, he certainly had few peers when it came to his winning ways exhibited in managing to place a diamond ring on three beautiful, accomplished women, making Trump, in some ways, both the most admired and envied man among men in America. "This focus on his athletic achievement is as much about establishing the man's interest in competition as it is about a desire to communicate some verifiable record," author Michael D'Antonio writes in *Never Enough.*

> Trump wants people to know that he always had the heart and the ability of a winner, and these claims come with certain proof. Trump can prove, too, that he has always been especially interested in attractive women. At (New York Military Academy), where hand-holding was forbidden, the cadets nevertheless identified him as the official 'ladies' man' of his class in the academy yearbook, appropriately titled *Shrapnel.*[15]

* * *

Ask a dozen people who have been entrenched in leadership positions for five years or more what they believe to be the three or four most important qualities (expressed in one or two words) in being a good leader, you will hear at least a couple dozen different answers. Most likely, all of them would be good answers, worth taking to heart if you are a leader wannabe or even in a managerial position for a company or other organization looking to get bumped up in that next promotion. Let's take a look at several of those leadership qualities to examine more closely how well Trump fares in those areas.

Teamwork

Legendary football coach Vince Lombardi, who coached the Green Bay Packers to victory in the first two Super Bowls, was the source of many great, memorable sayings, one of which was, "Individual commitment to a group effort—that is what makes a team work."[16] Put those last two words together and you get *teamwork.*

Trump never accomplished much of anything without the assistance and input of others, and a good leader is expected to make that team work together in a collaborative manner, even if it means sometimes replacing or moving "players." Trump was criticized for his relatively frequent change of staffers or cabinet members, but he is far from being alone in that regard. Bill Belichick, winner of six Super Bowls with the New England Patriots, is notorious for trading away or releasing at least several players almost every year in order to keep his team in peak competitive makeup and form. At the college level, there are many head coaches (such as the University of Alabama's Nick Saban) who replace assistant coaches almost at will in order to have the best minds and motivators on his staff. This same sort of replacement/release dynamic is a regular practice of coaches and managers across many sports as well as among businesses and other hierarchal organizations.

The goal is to have the best available personnel on your team regardless at what level you are with any team, business, or organization; the most important aspect of this is having everyone pulling on the same end of the rope and working in a truly collaborative, cooperative manner. Sometimes changes have to be made, and good leaders seeking the greater good are bold to act when circumstances call for a change. It also means supporting your team members when they are in your stead, and inspiring them toward a sense of camaraderie, loyalty, fellowship, and pride.

"I don't like firing anyone," Trump said, when asked about his longtime reality television show *The Apprentice*, where someone got fired at the end of each episode. His stated outlook is also reflective of his leadership style in the real world of business and government. He continued,

> Sometimes, it's necessary, but I'd rather keep people around me for a long time. I have employees who have been with me for over thirty years. The best working environment is when everyone has the same work ethic and focus and does their best. That's the case with most of my employees, but not always, and, if not, then a change has to be made.[17]

Trump also adds,

> If you can get a core group around you that you like and who understands your needs, you will be heading in the right direction. Sometimes I think it's divine intervention when the right people show up.... You have to give people a chance to prove themselves. But in the interim, it helps a lot if you like having them around to begin with.... Every person has unique talents that may or may not be in

their job description or listed on their resume . . . although I may be demanding, I am also fair. My door is always open, and they feel confident that when they have something to say, I'll be listening.[18]

Plugging the right people into the right spots in your organization is crucial to maintaining an optimal team, but it can be hit and miss. Things don't always work out. Trump has told the story of how he hired what he described as a "dynamic, very well-qualified, very well-educated young man." Trump, the business owner, was expecting great things of his new hire, but it didn't take him long to figure out he had made a bad hire. The young man couldn't explain things in a few words and his long-windedness was ill-suited for Trump's fast-paced management style and work environment, and the young man eventually left the organization. He wasn't a bad guy, just a bad fit.

On the other hand, Trump years ago once hired a project manager whose job description included collecting rent from tenants. In time, Trump realized that the man was intensely politically incorrect and also insulting around others—a con man, no less—but he was able to work quickly, effectively, and got things accomplished—like a knack for collecting rent from reluctant tenants, a job requirement that screams for a certain kind of art form. And this guy nailed it. "He got Swifton Village (one of Trump's development properties) running well enough so that I didn't have to be in Cincinnati very often," Trump said. "I knew he was probably ripping me off, but he kept the place well and people actually paid their rent. The project was a resounding success."[19]

One conclusion to be made about leadership is that a leader is only as effective and successful as his or her subordinates are in terms of embracing the mission and their respective roles. It also means being loyal to those to whom they answer, and being respectful of the man or woman in charge. Adds Phillips: "Those subordinates who will take risks, act without waiting for direction, and ask for responsibility rather than reject it, should be treated as your most prized possessions. Such individuals are exceedingly rare and worth their weight in gold."[20]

Vision/Inspiration

A leader with vision encompasses more than just good eyesight and, in modern times, the ability to see the traffic light in front of you at the intersection. It means being able to see the big picture where small snapshots are more readily present, as well as seeing beyond today; not just to tomorrow, but to the days, weeks, months and even years ahead. It means having a notion of how what you do today will affect your team, business, or organization in the long run.

Mike Huckabee, the former governor of Arkansas and twice a presidential candidate, says this: "A leader is the one who can outline the broad vision and the direction, and says here's where we are going to go, here's why we need to go there, and here's how we are going to get there."[21] Jack Welch, a former CEO at of General Electric (GE) added this: "Good business leaders create a vision, articulate the vision, passionately own the vision, and relentlessly drive it to completion."[22]

At Abraham Lincoln's first inauguration, in March 1861, a new iron dome was under construction atop the Capitol building but only half-completed, its naked ribs stretching skyward. Not much of a glorious look for a structure that supposedly represented the ideals of a nation, now about to go to war against itself. Debate raged about whether the building effort should continue. It was of exorbitant cost and, besides, the men who had been tasked to work on it were now becoming a part of the Union Army. Undeterred, Lincoln ordered the continuation of construction, saying that it was important, symbolically, that completing the task was something important. "If people see the Capitol going on, it is a sign we intend the Union shall go on," he said.[23]

That edict to continue the Capitol dome's rebuild was Lincoln's unspoken statement between the lines that he was a leader with vision, someone who could inspire others by having them identify with something larger than themselves, even an abstract representation of the nation's ideals. As Kearns Goodwin puts it, "Such leaders call for sacrifice in the pursuit of moral principles and higher goals, validating such altruism by looking beyond the present moment to frame a future worth striving for."[24]

It's almost impossible to determine when Donald Trump became a similar visionary. He's the ultimate outlier in Washington, DC, a forward-looking president who announced as he was taking office that his slogan and real intent was to make American great again and "drain the swamp" full of lifetime politicians who had an unspoken code and a long-entrenched manner of conducting business that didn't sit well with him.

Trump came to the White House stepping on toes and proclaiming an ambitious agenda, all geared toward improving the lives and restoring the patriotism of his followers. Washington got turned upside-down, and

Trump shook down the thunder. He saw a vision for America that was about building it up, not tearing it down and apologizing for America being America to the rest of the world as his predecessor had done.

"The Left and much of the media are horrified, because the age-old power structures on which they rely are specifically the ones President Trump is seeking to demolish and rebuild," Gingrich writes.

> Some in the establishment are confused, because Trump's campaign—and his first months in office—are totally opposite from business as usual in Washington. His success calls into question their (the mainstream media's, especially) presumed expertise and collective worldview. But many Americans are happy. To them President Trump represents a force of change in Washington, the likes of which we've rarely seen in American history.[25]

Trump takes it up a notch from there, explaining his vision and purpose for America:

> Leadership is leaders inducing followers to act for certain goals that represent the values and the motivations—the wants and needs, the aspirations and expectations—of both leaders and followers. And the genius of leadership lies in the manner in which leaders see and act on their own and their followers' values and motivations." [26]

In other words, make America great again!

* * *

Tammy Berberick, CEO of Crestcom International, writes, "The ability to lead through influence, rather than authority, is the most important quality of a great leader. Influence requires strong coaching, emotional intelligence, effective communication, negotiation, and consensus building skills."[27]

Having a great vision and being able to explain it to followers in a way that is understandable and grabs their attention is one thing. Getting those followers to act on it, though, is another matter. That's where motivation and inspiration come to the front of the line, and few politicians of the last hundred years have been better at doing that than Trump, whose ability to rally the masses in huge events is every bit as impressive as the hellfire preachers that America has seen and heard from over the last several centuries. Donald Trump Jr. says it well in describing how his dad can discern the best in people and push them to excel: "He has recognized the talent and the drive that all Americans have. He's promoted people based on their character, their street smarts, and their work ethic, not simply paper or credentials." Don Jr.'s sister Ivanka adds, "He showed us how to be resilient, how to deal with challenges, and how to strive for excellence in all that we do. He taught us that there's nothing that we cannot accomplish, if we marry vision and passion with an enduring work ethic."[28]

Decisiveness

Avid decision-making has always been a Trump hallmark, unlike the waiting and waffling exhibited by his immediate White House predecessors. "There is always the possibility of failure," Trump said, "but there is a greater chance of success if you actually try to do something versus doing nothing."[29]

While traditional mainstream media has often called them reckless and even dangerous, the decisions Trump has made from the White House could just as easily be termed decisive, bold, and—to borrow a pet phrase from Democrats—progressive. Putting America first and making America great again can be considered progress, right? Just a simple matter of perspective. Millions of liberal Americans and left-leaning media would disparage Trump even if he were to engineer the eradication of cancer and reduce unemployment to zero percent. His sin and the source of the scorn: his winning a 2016 presidential election that most media said he would, and should, lose; and his refusal to give up the fight to make America great again.

The list of Trump's significant bold and decisive actions as president is a long one, to include the following: greenlighting construction of the controversial Keystone XL Pipeline; establishing a sixth branch of the U.S. Armed Services, the Space Force; revising the U.S. tax code; issuing an executive order to promote excellence and innovation at historically black colleges and universities; ordering a cruise missile attack on Syrian base; killing terrorist leaders Abu Bakr al-Baghdadi and Qassem Soleimani; and firing FBI Director James Comey.

It's all part of the unique leadership formula that forms the constitution of who Donald Trump is and what he is capable of doing—driving himself to one finish line after another and challenging others to keep up, even if it means following in his wake.

It also means giving back. "What I admire most are people who put themselves directly on the line," Trump said back in his pre-political days as a businessman, and perhaps describing himself in the process.

I've never been terribly interested in why people give, because their motivation is rarely what it seems to be, and it's almost never pure altruism. To me, what matters is the doing, and giving time is far more valuable than just giving money.

In my life, there are two things I've found I'm very good at: overcoming obstacles and motivating good people to do their best work. One of the challenges ahead is how to use those skills as successfully in the service of others as I've done, up to now, on my own behalf. Don't get me wrong. I also plan to keep making deals, big deals, and right around the clock. [30]

There you have it, yet another dimension of leadership—Donald Trump: servant-leader.

Chapter Ten

A House Divided

"Now that the election is over, may not all, having a common interest,
reunite in a common effort, to save our common country?"

-Lincoln addresses a congratulatory serenade on his reelection,

Nov. 10, 1864

I T WAS A PRESIDENCY FILLED WITH PARTISAN STRIFE: A NOT-SO-SUBTLE
political bias emanating from much of the media, acts of violence in the
streets, constant chatter about plans and conspiracies to remove the president from office, bickering among members of both houses of Congress
that teetered on the brink of the outrageous, and all this in a country with
a citizenry arguably more divisive than it had been at any time in American
history.

Much of this was revved up even before he had been inaugurated, and it
reached a fever pitch within hours of his election that would carry throughout his first term in office, like a runaway locomotive. It was remarkable that Abraham Lincoln was able to get anything accomplished as the
White House's chief resident. That's the way it was in 1861, and history has
recently repeated itself, this time with Donald Trump wearing the target on
his back.

If the description in the previous paragraph sounded strikingly familiar
to anyone—there's good reason for it. Trump has had to endure the same
junk Lincoln weathered more than 150 years ago. The names, technology
and exact circumstances have changed, but all the rest? Instant replay. Like
Lincoln, Trump had been subjected to an ongoing assault for months before
taking office in January 2017. The incessant, derogatory attacks against
Trump's politics, his character, his family, his past business dealings, his
tax records, his fitness for office, his embrace of political incorrectness, his
reliance on and ample use of social media to get his message out to the
people—you name it, the hits just kept on coming. The animosity hit a

fever pitch in the early morning hours of November 10, 2016. This was after it became clear that he had surpassed the electoral vote threshold needed to beat Democratic nominee Hillary Clinton, whose shock at losing was as profound for her as it was for her supporters. The rampant bitterness of the Democrats showed itself in many ways, not to exclude Clinton's inability to concede publicly until well into the next day. Donald Trump was president, and he has been paying for it ever since.

Common paths and parallels between the Lincoln and Trump presidencies and parallels between the men themselves are most evident in the context of the divided nation in which they governed. Each man took office against the backdrop of politically chaotic environments. Each won elections with less than fifty percent of the popular vote.

It was Trump who quickly coined the phrase "fake news" to describe the un-journalistic practices of a slothful, slanted, sloppy mainstream media that clearly demonstrated its primary mission was not just to hammer away at "Orange Man" from every angle conceivable, but to make his life and presidency miserable. The end game was to push him out of office with U.S. House Speaker Nancy Pelosi leading the Democratic charge.

Lincoln had to deal with the same sort of sham media back in the nineteenth century. During this time the press played politics with an expertise even beyond twenty-first century news outlets. Democratic newspapers spouted Democratic ideology and solely supported their causes and candidates while castigating and condemning Republicans (and Lincoln.) Likewise, Republican papers embraced their own causes with the same targeted focus. Fair and balanced? Not in Lincoln's America! Within about a week after winning his first term, the following political "analysis" appeared in the November 13, 1860, edition of the Memphis Daily Appeal. Notice the open hostility dripping from the newspaper pages. Sound familiar? Just like Trump in 2016.

> Within 90 days from the time Lincoln is inaugurated (in March 1861), the Republican Party will be utterly ruined and destroyed. His path is environed with so many difficulties, that even if he had the ability of Jefferson and the energy of Jackson, he would fail, but he is a weak and inexperienced man, and his administration will be doomed from the commencement.[1]

Media hostility is nothing new for U.S. presidents, but the intensity that Trump had to deal with has little precedent in U.S. history, as former

U.S. Speaker of the House and current political pundit Newt Gingrich describes:

> The intensity of the media's hostility to President Trump resembles the media reaction to Presidents Andrew Jackson, Abraham Lincoln, and Franklin Delano Roosevelt. When a president comes along who challenges existing orthodoxies and power structures, he or she has to be ready for vicious, intense condemnation from those currently in power.[2]

There were also the public protests, some taking place simply because of a hate for Lincoln, and others with more of a policy bend to them—namely, Lincoln's stated desire to abolish slavery, a stance that didn't sit well with southerners, more specifically southern Democrats. The Democratic Party of the nineteenth century (and well into the twentieth century) was the pro-slavery party, just as it would be the anti-civil rights party of the 1950s and 1960s—a fact that present-day liberal Dems will either deny or rationalize

Following is a newspaper clipping from that era, presented by Newt Gingrich in *Understanding Trump*. It talks about the protests and other indications of the political and public tensions of the time. Again, keep in mind, this is about Lincoln and the 1860s, even though it could easily be applied to Trump in the twenty-first century:

This is from the Lancaster Ledger (a South Carolina paper), and it was published in November 1860: "There is intense excitement here. Large crowds have gathered in the streets. The pervading spirit among the masses is resistance to Lincoln's administration [which was still four months away!]"[3]

Gingrich draws a parallel between South Carolinians who were pushing for secession in defense of slavery and twenty-first century liberal Democrat activists protesting Trump's bold plan for making America great again. There was no real purpose to protesting Trump, no specific issue to zero in on, other than the fact that he was still breathing and the protestors hated him. Trump's biggest sins were his general endorsement of conservatism and having the gall to beat an entitled Hillary Clinton in the 2016 presidential election.

Among historians and students of history, Lincoln's tenure as U.S. president is most closely associated with slavery and the Civil War. But rising tensions at the time were an outgrowth of major demographic and industrial shifts that were radically changing America, pulling the national consciousness in different, sometimes divisive directions.

"Lincoln was troubled by what he perceived as the rapid change in American life," Donald writes.

> Canals and railroads were bringing about a transportation revolution; the population was swiftly spreading across the continent; immigration was beginning to seem a threat to American social cohesion; sectionalism was becoming ever more divisive as the controversy over slavery mounted; (and) the political battles of the Jackson era had destroyed the national political consensus.[4]

The Trump years had similarly potent forces pulling U.S. citizens apart, leaving us with a citizenry where tempers are short, distrust is high, and, in so many ways, we are surrounded by endless piles of dry kindling. A single spark can set off a firestorm that always seems to end up at the feet of Donald Trump. In place of canals and railroads and a massive westward migration of the populace, the world before and under Trump was best illuminated by the explosion of digital technology and social media.

The results were major breakdowns in human interaction and communication; major economic shifts, centered around a diminishing middle class; identity politics whose flames were lit and abetted by America's first black president; a growing secularization of a nation that was founded on the principles of a Judeo-Christian faith now being gradually replaced by a humanism that has no room for God and the Ten Commandments. We also saw a shifting awareness in which Americans increasingly lost touch with traditional values and morals. These values are now being rooted out of our fabric and gradually replaced by the normalization of socialistic mores in a way that just several decades ago would have been considered reprehensible.

All this explains why half of America sees Trump as the savior and restorer of what once made America great while the other half sees him as the ultimate enemy of the state. That's how twisted our nation has become, as wrong now assumes the role of right. Along with that, the Deep State has now made Trump out to be an Enemy of the State. Those powerful forces were aligned against Trump throughout his presidency, and even continued their onslaught against citizen Trump, not just to knock him out, but to keep him down for the count.

Another thing that is not well known about Lincoln, but that makes his ties to Trump even stronger—he was disliked, even disdained by many of his political contemporaries, including members of his own political party. "Liberal Republicans thought he was too calculating, too quick to weigh public opinion. Democrats thought he was a tyrant, a rube, and was destroying the Constitution [in today's world that would truly be the pot calling the kettle black]," says Edward Achorn, author of *Every Drop of Blood: The Momentous Second Inauguration of Abraham Lincoln.*

> I think a lot of this was airbrushed out of history after he was assassinated, when he became a martyr. But when you go back to that day and look at what people were saying, you get a stunning sense of what Lincoln was up against. There's a lot of hostility from all sides. I'm not sure how he withstood it.[5]

Here's another angle to the Lincoln-Trump connection. In both eras violence in the streets and mob behavior was initiated by and carried out by groups politically opposed to the sitting president–Lincoln's election touched off a firestorm of protests and public unrest in the southern slave-holding states fueling already smoldering resentments that were leading toward secession.[6] Though this violence was publicly supported by politicians on the opposite side of the aisle, it is the president who gets blamed. It's a head scratcher.

In spring-summer 2020, BLM-led protests that turned into riots and rampant destruction (buildings and businesses burned, bystanders and homeowners attacked, police assaulted—the usual tactics of tolerant "progressives") occurred most notably in cities such as Minneapolis, Chicago, Atlanta, Seattle, and Portland—all with Democratic mayors who essentially allowed the violence to continue by taking a hands-off approach in law enforcement and refusing to condemn the attacks. They also adamantly opposed any intervention by federal officials to quell the riots. On top of all that, it was reported that at least thirteen members of Biden's 2020 campaign team made donations to the Minnesota Freedom Fund,[8] which used contributions to bail out protesters or rioters who had been arrested in the wake of the Floyd death. Wrong was right, and, still, the blame went against Trump, the Republican president.

Lincoln, like Trump, knew what it was like to be tagged with blame for protests and riots that were against him. At times it was the media itself that did the blaming. Case in point: the New York City draft riots in July

1863 featured violent disturbances in lower Manhattan in the wake of new laws passed by the U.S. Congress that greenlighted the drafting of men to fight in the Civil War. The press called Lincoln a "tyrant" and a "dictator." When they don't know what to speak and which words to use to properly express their beliefs, that's all that angry contrarians can manage to say.[7]

Early in the summer of 1858, two years before he was elected to the presidency, Lincoln gave one of his most memorable speeches—second perhaps in notoriety only to his Gettysburg Address of 1863—in which he said, "A house divided against itself cannot stand." Although criticized at the time, the speech remains noteworthy 150-plus years later for its prophetic accuracy in predicting what would become of the United States three years later with the breakout of the Civil War. "A House Divided" took on almost mythical status for its applicability to a divided nation, and it gets added credence today because of how it applies to where America stood headed into the 2020 and the 2024 elections. Not since the days of Lincoln and slavery had America been so angrily at odds along politically partisan lines, with little, if any, middle ground for compromise.

This twenty-first century divisiveness didn't start with Trump's election in 2016. This latest edition of extreme partisanship dates back at least to the controversial presidential election of 2000. That's when George W. Bush was edged out in the national popular vote by his Democratic rival Al Gore, Jr. but won a narrow Electoral College victory that wasn't decided until weeks later. The U.S. Supreme Court finally ruled the vote recount in Florida over, its razor-thin advantage for Bush giving him the last slice of electoral votes he needed to squeak past Gore in an election that left Democrats bitter and claiming they had been robbed.

It was a similar deal sixteen years later, when Hillary Clinton won the national popular vote, only for Trump to narrowly win several key battleground states, allowing him to upset Clinton. However, Trump finished with a comparatively comfortable margin in the Electoral College count. It was a bitter loss for Clinton and Democrats, and they didn't bother hiding their shock at the loss and their utter contempt for Trump the president as well as Trump the man. Conservatives and others who supported Trump had no pity for the defeated Clinton and Democrats—they had had to put up with eight years of Barack Obama's two-term reign as America's Liberal in Chief. Obama made identity politics a cornerstone of his administration and set America on a course toward socialism. Obama fanned the partisan flames by saying it was time for America to redistribute the wealth, by following an economic model that is the basis for communism, and by showing a hands-off approach toward Islamic extremism and terrorism, as evidenced through his consistent reluctance to even mention those terms.

America's electoral election of Trump was an act of defiance against the political correctness movement that had flourished under the Obama/Biden administration; Trump wasted no time in declaring his "Make America Great Again" (MAGA) commitment after announcing his run for the presidency. He quickly amassed a loyal following of ordinary people sold on his vision for America. It's worth noting that a century and a half earlier, Lincoln had had his own take on an "America Great" mission statement, one in which he proposed to "motivate and mobilize followers by persuading them to take ownership of their roles in a more grand mission," as Donald T. Phillips wrote in his book *Lincoln on Leadership*. Phillips elaborates further, writing,

> Lincoln's grand mission, his 'common purpose,' was essentially the American experiment and the ideals expressed in the Declaration of Independence. He aimed at the 'elevation of men,' opposed anything that tended to degrade them, and especially lashed out at the institution of slavery... He lifted people out of their everyday selves and into a higher level of performance, achievement, and awareness. He obtained extraordinary results from ordinary people by instilling purpose in their endeavors."[8]

While running for office in 2016, Trump quickly showed he wasn't expecting mainstream media to help him to get his message out to the public. Instead he defied the established media elite by launching his own media apparatus through countless TV appearances. Any televised appearance by Trump at one of his rallies was catnip to networks and stations subservient to ratings. Even more conspicuously, he ambitiously and creatively used social media—particularly Twitter during his presidency and then later his own platform launched in 2021, Truth Social—to get his messages out with full impact and without filter.

The prize fight was on: Donald Trump in his corner, his many detractors in another. Here's how Gingrich, writing in 2018, around the midpoint of Trump's first term, described the dynamic between Trump and whatever parts of the country opposed him:

For decades, this conflict has been fought quietly in city halls, classrooms, school boards, courtrooms, town squares, and state houses across the country. However, the election of President Trump has clarified the battle lines in this struggle and elevated these individual fights into a united national conflict.

On one side of this conflict is a factional anti-Trump coalition—a strange amalgam of radicals, liberals, globalists, establishment elites from both parties, and blatantly anti-American groups loosely held together by their hostility and disdain for the president. On the other side is Trump's America—the millions of hardworking people who are united by respect for our foundational freedoms, traditional values, and history of limited commonsense governance.[9]

The anti-Trumpers didn't waste any time mounting their charges against the new president, insisting with zero evidence that he was a tyrant-in-waiting set to destroy America, when in fact Trump was here to clean up a mess that had festered under eight years of an Obama Administration. Nationwide, liberals had praised the Obama presidency, some even ranking him the greatest U.S. president of all time, but for what? Certainly not for making America better. Americans who'd had their eyes open for those eight years had watched in anger, and horror, as the federal government took and then squandered tax dollars, ruining America's businesses, and making it much harder to earn a decent living. Still, in the eyes of liberals, Trump had "stolen" the election. For good measure, they hatched a Russian collusion story, giving Democrats hope that the election could soon be overturned—if only their ludicrous charges had any truth to them.

Inauguration Day in January 2017 brought out the dichotomy in twenty-first century America as both sides showed up to witness Trump being sworn in as forty-fifth president of the United States. On one side of the spectrum were diehard Republicans and Trump supporters, many conspicuously wearing their bright red MAGA hats, streaming out of their hotels in Washington, D.C. to make their way to the U.S. Capitol grounds to see Trump sworn in by Supreme Court Chief Justice John Roberts.

"Then the other America showed up—the one that blocked people from entering checkpoints to the Capitol grounds, harassed Trump supporters, set cars on fire, smashed storefronts, and hurled rocks at police," Gingrich says.

CNN reported the following day that six police officers were injured and 217 protestors arrested after 'ugly street clashes in downtown Washington.'

Much of the news media covered the weekend with nothing short of vindictiveness. Instead of pointing out how gracefully the supporters at the Capitol handled being confronted with virulent hate and vulgarity from the Left (no Trump supporters were arrested), the media decided to focus on how big the crowd was compared with past inaugurations.[10]

Deflection, filled with untruths.

It wasn't just in D.C. that this anti-Trump-motivated civil unrest—to put a diplomatic spin on it—was taking place. During the weekend of the inauguration, other locales in which police arrested violent left-wing protesters included New York, Dallas, Chicago, Portland, and Seattle. Gingrich adds,

In Oregon, the protestors were armed with clubs, setting fire to American flags, and throwing rocks, bottles, and flares at police, according to local news reports. Protestors at the University of Washington campus threw bricks at officers. But according to the Left, it's the Trump supporters who are hateful, closed-minded, and dangerous... But as a very senior former prosecutor said to me recently, "This has now become a blood sport. The goal is not justice or truth, the goal is destruction of conservatives."[11]

At the time of Trump's election in 2016 and then his inauguration, the biggest issue dividing America was Trump himself. His supporters embraced him because he was a Beltway outsider willing to make positive changes in America, while Trump haters hated him, well, just because he was there. To support their discrediting of Trump, they fabricated and twisted narratives about him, loading them with inaccurate generalities and other falsehoods that, when parroted by a compliant media, gained momentum in the avenues of public discourse, growing into misleading talking points that were continually tweaked and augmented over the next four years and beyond.

Lincoln also had two opposite Americas to deal with. In his time, it was slavery that divided the nation. It all came down to something Lincoln once wrote, summing up where things stood with these words: "You think slavery is right . . . and we think it is wrong."[12] Abraham Lincoln had the nerve to challenge the Democratic forces promoting the expansion and permanence of slavery in America.

The similarities between Lincoln's first inauguration speech in 1860 and Trump's inaugural valedictory of 2016 are worth noting, both for their shared tone of forceful clarity and for the common topics of their respective messages. "Both were clear statements of nonnegotiable principles to bitter opposition, both had survived some of the most divisive campaigns in American history, and both appealed to patriotism," Gingrich writes.[13] He asked Dr. Allen Guelzo, Lincoln historian and the director of Civil War Studies Program at Gettysburg College at the time, for a second opinion. Guelzo replied,

> Your points are entirely on the mark. I have done a quick comparative outline of both inaugural addresses, and while the existential situation of the two are different . . . there is this common thread, the sovereignty of the people. Lincoln used that principle to deny that one part of the nation, the seven seceding states, could break up the union, without the consent of the American people, as well as denying that one branch of the government, the Supreme Court, could overrule the American's people will . . . Trump invoked that principle. To deny that, a federal bureaucracy can enrich and empower itself at the expense of the people, as well as denying that identity enclaves can overrule the fundamental unity of the American people . . . America is deeply divided along a political-cultural fault line. One side wants to see America return to prosperity, strength, and its traditional values. The other wants to fundamentally change America into a different nation that rejects many of its founding principles.[14]

What we now have, like we did in 1860, is an ideological divide that was widened by Trump's election. Trump was not personally responsible for that, but his election and later his presidency touched off a liberal outrage that was poised and predictable, fueled by the likes of Clinton. During her presidential campaign, she had fed into Democrats' biases by describing half of Trump's supporters as "deplorables," who were "racist, sexist, homophobic, xenophobic, Islamophobic—you name it," adding on that all that made them "irredeemable."[15] The intensity of the national divide has continued to climb ever since along the lines of what Dennis Prager wrote in a National Review op-ed that ran in January 2017. In it, he declared that we were in an American Civil War, not one fought on soil or the water or in the air (at least not yet), but one on political and ideological grounds. [16]

Again, we turn to Gingrich for a description of the angry-liberal outrage that has been a thorn in Trump's side longer than the four years he was in office:

> The Left was dealt a strong blow by the 2016 election. It was stunned for a moment but has recovered, ready to continue its ideological war . . . The hyper-Left wants to create an America that's unacceptable to the vast majority of Americans . . . they focus on insidiously divisive identity politics, branding all Republicans as racist, and keeping Americans dependent on the government . . . Yet the hard Left can't solve anything. The Left has no solutions for Chicago's violence, West Virginia's poverty, or disastrous schools in Baltimore. All they can do is yell 'racism!' and 'sexism!' and hope that holds their coalition together.[17]

* * *

One hundred fifty years ago, the pro-slavery Democrats embraced the plantation mentality. That's how they kept the reins on their black servants, holding them as slaves and mostly treating them as less than human. The existence and well-being of slaves was almost wholly dependent on the will, attention, and generosity of their white owners. Now, twenty-plus years deep into the twenty-first century, nothing much has changed except much of the Dems' plantations have been moved from the agrarian South to the urban jungles of cities across America. And now tax-obsessed Democrats keep many unwitting voters dependent on them for welfare and other government entitlements and handouts. In return, the Dems—through political cunning and patronization—are paid back through overwhelming ballot-box loyalty from these modern-day slaves, who come in an assortment of ethnicities, some with questionable citizenship. Chalk one up for today's socialist state administered by the all-powerful Liberal elites. This is progressivism hard at work, right? Well, here's what's really at work: the more things change, the more they remain the same.

Lincoln served as president in a world where the plantation mentality was a potent political force, and so it was in our day with Donald Trump in office. We see the ties that bind together two presidents a century and a half apart. At stake was and is America's future existence, which goes well beyond just which political party happens to be in charge at any given time. In his Lyceum Address in 1838, Lincoln suggested that if America ever ceased to exist, it would perish through internal ruin, not from an attack by a foreign power. "Shall we expect some transatlantic military giant to step the Ocean, and crush us at a blow? Never! . . . If destruction be our lot, we must ourselves be its author and finisher. As a nation of freemen, we must live through all time, or die by suicide." [18]

Here's one way how the twenty-first century works as it did on the plantations. If you step out of line and try to expose—or even succeed in exposing—the true workings, agendas, and goals of the Liberal state, also known as socialism, you will incur the wrath of the Democratic Deep State. That's what happened to best-selling author, political commentator, and filmmaker Dinesh D'Souza. Here's part of his story, in his own words:

> A few years ago, I witnessed a determined, ruthless effort to kill my American dream. Shortly after I released a highly successful film criticizing Barack Obama, the FBI came banging on my door. Soon I discovered that Preet Bharara, the prosecuting attorney for the Southern District of New York, had charged me with violating campaign finance laws. My heinous offense was to give $20,000 of my own money to a longtime college friend of mine running a quixotic campaign for U.S. Senate in New York.[19]

He was charged with a felony and found guilty. D'Souza was sentenced to eight months of overnight confinement at a halfway house, where his dormitory confinement kept him in a bunk bed in proximity to sixty hardened federal felons. He also had to pay a fine, perform community service, and serve out five years of probation. From D'Souza's perspective, he was a nonwhite immigrant born the same year as Obama (1961), but he saw an America different from the one that Obama viewed. D'Souza believed that the forty-fourth president wanted to remake America into a socialist state, one that killed the American dream for a well-educated immigrant such as himself. [20]

He continues, tying in his dream to the visions of Abraham Lincoln:

> Such a death would involve not only the collapse of America's founding principles but also the extinction of its characteristic mores and values and what Lincoln termed its 'mystic chords of memory.' In effect, we'd still have the American people, but they would no longer bear the recognizable American stamp. They—we—would

no longer dream American dreams. The America that I and so many of my fellow Americans have come to love would no longer exist.[21]

In the early part of the nineteenth century, there were an abundance of antislavery forces in the South, numbering more than a hundred organizations intent on ending slavery. They included in their ranks planters who regarded such bondage as immoral, and they were joined by church leaders. But public sentiment, mostly among Democrats in the South and in some parts of the North, began to shift. By the 1830s, according to historian Stanley Elkins, "the hostility to slavery that had been common in Jeffersonian times . . . all but disappeared." According to John Blasingame, writing in a publication called *The Slave Community*, "By the 1840s, the propagandists had largely succeeded in silencing the [antislavery] churches." Not only that, but clergy were being persistently pressured into becoming advocates of slavery, and many caved. 22

As D'Souza points out, planters initiated a mostly successful campaign to prevent antislavery literature from being distributed via mail. Besides that, every southern state other than Maryland and Kentucky passed laws prohibiting the teaching of reading and writing to slaves. Just like today's PC culture trumpeted by Democrats, a "cancel culture" was in place before Lincoln moved into the White House. By the 1850s there was even talk of reopening the African slave trade. All things considered, the time and circumstances were ripe for the Democratic Party to step in and enthusiastically align themselves with the slave proponents. Democrats were eager to represent their interests and press their claims, as D'Souza puts it, at the local level as well as at the national level. This became a cultural and political match made in political correctness heaven, with the Democrats now manipulating the puppet strings. At this point the doctrine of "popular sovereignty," whereby northern Democrats would do their part to protect and grow slavery, was "one equally imbued with racism and one that identified the cause of slavery with the cause of democracy itself." 23

When Trump rails against things such as the "deep state," "draining the swamp," and even "fake news," this is sort of the thing he is talking about. More specifically, "The past has not disappeared from the present," D'Souza writes.

There is an important difference between the old Democratic plantation and the new one. The old one was based on forced black labor; the new one is based on the dependent black, Latino, or Native

American voter. The voter ideally does not work but rather lives off welfare and government provision, which becomes, of course, his motive to sustain the providing party in power. Democrats use coalitions of dependent ethnic minorities in order to generate an electoral majority, thus placing progressive Democrats in charge of the Big House.[24]

Part of Lincoln's legacy to his successors—and that would eventually include Trump—was a staunch determination to take on the Democratic plantation, as D'Souza puts it. The fact that Trump was a political outsider, just as Lincoln had been, made them the right men for the job. It's also interesting to note that Lincoln and Trump shared a dislike of Democrats and disrespect for the Left, with Lincoln expressing his scorn for them by calling them names such as "Locofocos" and Mobocrats," while Trump preferred just to outright call them "stone cold crazy."

Other descriptions Lincoln assigned to pro-slavery Democrats indirectly referred to them as "skunks" and "evil." In 1859, he gave more than a dozen talks across the Midwest in which he focused his attacks on slavery, hoping to stimulate open discussion about it across the country. "Slavery is doomed, and that within a few years," he said to an audience in Columbus, Ohio. "Evil can't stand discussion . . . What kills the skunk is the publicity it gives itself. What a skunk wants to do is keep snug under the barn in the daytime, when men are around with shotguns."[25]

It's no wonder that Trump went into the 2020 presidential election often voicing his concerns about the legitimacy of the election process, mindful of the dirty tricks and apparent election rigging Democrats had allegedly been engaged in for decades, if not for hundreds of years. Inside his chapter entitled "Urban Plantation" from his book *Death of a Nation*, D'Souza talks about bygone days (not so "bygone" actually) in which Democratic bosses "controlled political appointments and the dispensing of patronage; they also controlled the voting process. In several cities, including New York, the bosses didn't rely on immigrants to vote correctly. Rather, they supplied the immigrants with filled-in ballots."[26]

This is how it worked back then: when immigrants showed up at polling places to cast their votes, they would be handed a blank ballot and then, when the voting monitor wasn't looking, the filled-in ballot would be substituted for the blank ballot and cast, assuring favorable outcomes for the Democratic bosses.

"As the machines grew established, they also grew bolder, now going beyond filled-in votes to also deliver dead people's votes in favor of Democratic machine candidates," D'Souza writes. "The ethnic exploitation of vulnerable people and the callous use of their votes to rip off the general population are somehow presented as triumphs of democratic inclusion."[27]

This is how the Democratic machine controls the voting process in today's modern elections: first, key Democrat-run battleground states pause vote counting in the heaviest populated cities in the middle of the night. Then, a variety of new and creative methods are employed to add votes until the desired candidate pulls ahead, and only then is the race called. It is important to mention, Democratic shenanigans were made easier in the 2020 election by an opportunistic political party machine taking full advantage of the confusion and fear of a national health crisis—the Coronavirus pandemic. Such "creative" vote-getting includes:

- Harvesting nursing home ballots

- Loading drop boxes with the "right" ballots by paid ballot traffickers (called "mules")

- Secretly injecting into the vote count stacks of pre-marked, pristine ballots with no envelopes or chain of custody

- Manipulating electronic voting machines and tabulators to either confuse the system or produce a desired outcome.

- Counting ballots multiple times

- Intentionally obfuscating recounts and audits making them too confusing to effectively challenge

- Delaying post-election reconciliation processes to ensure that large (or impossible) voter-to-vote discrepancies are not apparent until it's too late.[28]

And to top it all off, there are the "immigrants" enticed and admitted into the country en masse via an open southern border and expected to vote in the future for the Democratic candidates— Democratic "ethnic exploitation of vulnerable people" all over again. Just like the good old days.

Aside from voting "irregularities," to put it nicely, there has long been a Democratic Party practice of creating false narratives about the likes of

Lincoln (yes, even back then) as well as Trump. It's an old story. Truth has no room in the progressive playbook.

"Lincoln was portrayed by the Democrats and their allies, just as Trump is now, as being a grave threat to their fundamental liberties," D'Souza says.

> Yet we may ask about Trump the same question that Lincoln asked about himself. Has Trump actually violated any of the basic constitutional rights of his opponent? Has he deprived them of their free speech or the right to assemble or vote? No, he has not. And yet they persist in trying to drive him from office for the same reason their Democratic forbears sought to bring Lincoln to his knees, because they cannot abide the result of a free election.[29]

In a special message to Congress on July 4, 1861—two months into the Civil War—Lincoln spelled out what was really at stake:

> Our popular government has often been called an experiment. Two points in it our people have already settled—the successful establishing and the successful administering of it. One still remains—its successful maintenance against a formidable internal attempt to overthrow it.[30]

The relevancy of this remaining point was clear in Abraham Lincoln's America—a divided nation attacking each other on literal battlefields. The southern Democrats were knocked flat but not out in 1865 when their surrender to Union forces ended the American Civil War. Fast forward 150 years. The Democratic Party has come full circle. This formidable internal force rages in Donald Trump's America. A divided nation once again comes to blows in a very different kind of war. It's subversive, relentless. But not at all civil.

Notes

Chapter One An American Tale

1. Gwenda Blair, *The Trumps: Three Generations That Built an Empire* (New York: Simon and Schuster, 2000), 25.

2. Blair, *The Trumps*, 90–93.

3. Blair, 116.

4. Blair, 116–17.

5. Donald Trump, *The Art of the Deal* (New York: Ballantine Books, 1987), 33.

6. Donald J. Trump, *Great Again: How to Fix Our Crippled America* (New York: Threshold Editions, 2015), 128.

7. Donald Trump, The Art of the Deal (New York: Ballantine Books, 1987), 66.

8. Blair, 218.

9. Newt Gingrich, *Understanding Trump* (New York: Center Street, 2017), 133.

10. Blair, 228–29.

11. David Brody and Scott Lamb, *The Faith of Donald J. Trump: A Spiritual Biography.* (New York: Broadside Books, 2018), 14–15.

12. Trump, Art of the Deal, 67.

13. Donald J. Trump, *Great Again: How to Fix Our Crippled America* (New York: Threshold Editions, 2015), 128.

14. D'Antonio, *Never Enough*, 23.

15. Trump, *Art of the Deal*, 79.

16. Trump, *Art of the Deal*, 78.

17. Trump, *Great Again*, 128.

18. Dinesh D'Souza, *Death of a Nation: Plantation Politics and the Making of the Democratic Party* (New York: All Points Books, 2018), 71.

19. Trump, *Great Again*, 128.

20. Gingrich, *Understanding Trump*, 4

21. Michael D'Antonio, *Never Enough: Donald Trump and the Pursuit of Success* (New York: Thomas Dunne Books, 2015), 36.

22. D'Antonio, 46.

23. Blair, 225.

24. Trump, *Art of the Deal,* 80.

25. Donald J. Trump, *Think Like a Champion: An Informal Education in Business and Life* (New York: RP Minis, 2010), 59.

26. Newt Gingrich, *Trump's America* (New York: Center Street, 2018), 46.

27. Brody and Lamb, 174.

Chapter Two Simple Faith

1. Newt Gingrich, *Trump's America* (New York: Center Street, 2018), 46.

2. David Brody and Scott Lamb, *The Faith of Donald J. Trump: A Spiritual Biography* (New York: Broadside Books, 2018), 73.

3. Brody and Lamb, 65.

4. Brody and Lamb, 73.

5. Emma Green, "Trump's Sunday School," *The Atlantic,* July 24, 2016.

6. Green, "Trump's Sunday School."

7. Brody and Lamb, 76–77.

8. Dalia Fahmy, "Most Americans Don't See Trump as Religious; Fewer Than Half Say They Think He's Christian," Pew Research Center, March 25, 2020.

9. Pew Research Center, "Our History," https://www.pewresearch.org/ about/our-history/, viewed April 23, 2020.

10. Fahmy, "Most Americans Don't See Trump as Religious; Fewer Than Half Say They Think He's Christian."

11. Samuel Benson, "Most Republicans think Donald Trump is a person of faith. We asked why." Deseret News, January 3, 2024. https://www.deseret.com/2024/1/3/23982720/republicans-think-donald-trump-is-person-of-faith-we-asked-why/, viewed March 1, 2024.

12. Kelsey Dallas, "Trump, religion and the power of asking 'Why?'" January 9, 2024, https://www.deseret.com/faith/2024/1/9/24023895/trump-religion-why-evangelicals-support/, viewed March 1, 2024.

13. Bible, Matthew 7: 17.

14. Gwenda Blair, *The Trumps: Three Generations That Built an Empire* (New York: Simon and Schuster, 2000), 301.

15. Donald J. Trump, *Think Like a Champion: An Informal Education in Business and Life* (New York: RP Minis, 2010), 115.

16. Brody and Lamb, 290.

17. Brody and Lamb, 251.

18. Benjamin Fearnow, "Trump's Spiritual Advisor Paula White Appeals to Christians to Give to the Church Before Paying Mortgages, Electric Bills," Newsweek, February 18, 2020.

19. Brody and Lamb, 138.

20. Brody and Lamb, 406.

21. Brody and Lamb, 286.

22. Brody and Lamb, 209.

23. Brody and Lamb, 192.

24. Brody and Lamb, 203.

25. Brody and Lamb, 236.

26. Brody and Lamb, 235.

27. Brody and Lamb, 185.

28. Brody and Lamb, 266.

29. Newt Gingrich, Trump's America. (New York: Center Street, 2018, 56)

30. Brody and Lamb, 259.

31. Brody and Lamb, 301

Chapter Three Prizefighter

1. Gregg Re, "Trump, at Fox News Town Hall, Suggests Biden Isn't Competent: 'There's Something Going On There,' " Fox News, March 5, 2020, https://www.foxnews.com/politics/trump-fox-news-town-hall, viewed March 5, 2020.

2. Daniel Kurt, "Donald Trump's Success Story," Investopedia, July 7, 2019, https://www.investopedia.com/updates/donald-trump-success-story/, viewed March 6, 2020.

3. Bill O'Reilly, *The United States of Trump: How the President Really Sees America* (New York: Henry Holt and Company, 2019), xi.

4. Glenn Plaskin, "The Playboy Interview with Donald Trump," Playboy, March 1990, https://www.playboy.com/read/playboy-interviewdonald-trump-1990, viewed March 3, 2020.

5. O'Reilly, *The United States of Trump*, 16–17.

6. Gwenda Blair, *The Trumps: Three Generations That Built an Empire* (New York: Simon & Schuster, 2000), 238.

7. Michael D'Antonio, *Never Enough: Donald Trump and the Pursuit of Success* (New York: Thomas Dunne Books, 2015), 59.

8. Blair, 270.

9. Blair, 270–71.

10. Blair, 272.

11. Blair, 276.

12. Blair, 275–77.

13. Blair, 277.

14. Blair, 278.

15. Daniel Kurt, Investopedia. "Donald Trump's Success Story."

16. David Brody and Scott Lamb, *The Faith of Donald J. Trump* (New York: Broadside Books, 2018), 120.

17. Blair, 266.

18. O'Reilly, 144.

19. O'Reilly, 145.

20. Adam Edelman. "Trump Says NFL Players Who Kneel During National Anthem 'Maybe Shouldn't Be in the Country,'" nbcnews.com, May 24, 2018, https://www.nbcnews.com/politics/donald-trump/trumpsays-nf l-players-who-kneel-duringnational-anthem-maybe-n876996, viewed March 8, 2020.

21. John Fritze and David Jackson, "Donald Trump Reacts to Robert Mueller's First Public Statement: 'Case is Closed!'" USA Today, May 29, 2019, https://www.usatoday.com/story/news/politics/2019/05/29/donaldtrump-reacts-robert-muellers-statement-case-closed/1269744001/ , viewed March 8, 2020.

22. Dan Mangan, "Trump Says Democrats 'Not Nice!' for Holding Impeachment Hearings While He's Overseas—but GOP Did Same to Clinton," cnbc.com, December 2, 2019, https://www.cnbc.com/2019/12/02/trump-criticizes-democrats-for-impeachment-timing.html , viewed March 8, 2020.

23. Kathryn Watson, "Trump's margin of victory in Iowa GOP caucuses smashed previous record," cbsnews.com, January 16, 2024, https://www.cbsnews.com/news/trump-iowa-caucus-margin-of-victory/, viewed March 21, 2024.

24. Jack Izzo, "Is Trump the 1st Presidential Candidate in History To Win New Hampshire's Primary 3 Times?" snopes.com, Jan. 24, 2024, https://www.snopes.com/fact-check/trump-new-hampshire-primary-record/, viewed March 21, 2024.

25. Donald J. Trump, *Time to Get Tough* (Washington DC: Regnery Publishing, Inc., 2011), 165.

Chapter Four Uncommonly Common

1. Dinesh D'Souza, *Death of a Nation: Plantation Politics and the Making of the Democratic Party* (New York: All Points Books, 2018), 258.

2. Gene Ho, *Trumpography: How Biblical Principles Paved the Way to the American Presidency.* (iUniverse, 2018), 146.

3. Ho, *Trumpography*, 146.

4. Donald J. Trump, *Great Again: How to Fix Our Crippled America* (New York: Threshold Editions, 2015), 29.

5. Donald J. Trump. *Think Like a Champion: An Informal Education in Business and Life* (New York: RP Minis, 2010), 63.

6. Trump. *Think Like a Champion*, 63.

7. Trump, *Think Like a Champion*, 63.

8. David Brody and Scott Lamb, *The Faith of Donald J. Trump: A Spiritual Biography* (New York: Broadside Books, 2018), 125.

9. Brody and Lamb, *The Faith of Donald J. Trump*, 169.

10. Brody and Lamb, 172.

11. Joanna Weiss, "Trump Pokes Fun at Himself. Why Do Only Some People See It?" Politico Magazine, November 9, 2019.

12. Newt Gingrich, *Trump's America* (New York: Center Street, 2018), 91.

13. Newt Gingrich, *Understanding Trump* (New York: Center Street,2017), 43.

14. Andrew Restuccia and Ben Schreckinger, "In MAGA World, Trump's Jokes Always Land," www.politico.com, October 19, 2018.

15. Ho, *Trumpography*, 102.

16. Donald J. Trump with Meredith McIver, *Never Give Up: How I Turned My Biggest Challenges into Success* (New York: Wiley, 2008), 90.

Chapter Five All In the Family

1. David Brody and Scott Lamb, *The Faith of Donald J. Trump.* (New York: Broadside Books, 2018), 122.

2. Gwenda Blair, *The Trumps: Three Generations That Built an Empire* (New York: Simon and Schuster, 2000), 298.

3. Blair, *The Trumps*, 299.

4. Blair, 302-303.

5. Ivana Trump, *Raising Trump* (New York: Gallery Books, 2017), 5.

6. Bill O'Reilly, *The United States of Trump: How the President Really Sees America* (New York: Henry Holt and Company, 2019), 68.

7. O'Reilly, *The United States of Trump*, 68–69.

8. Donald J. Trump, *Great Again: How to Fix Our Crippled America* (New York: Threshold Editions, 2015), 129.

9. Ivana Trump, *Raising Trump* (New York: Gallery Books, 2017),2–3.

10. Gwenda Blair, *The Trumps: Three Generations That Built an Empire* (New York: Simon and Schuster, 2000), 399.

11. Blair, 399.

12. O'Reilly, 242.

13. Bethania Palma, "Is Melania Trump Fluent in Five Languages?", Snopes, December 30, 2019, https://www.snopes.com/fact-check/melaniatrump-multiple-languages/, viewed July 3, 2020.

14. Gabriella Paiella, "Melania Trump's Daily Mail Lawsuit Settled for $2.9 Million," The Cut, April 12, 2017, https://www.thecut. com/2017/04/melania-trumps-daily-mail-lawsuit-settled-usd2-9-million.html, viewed July 3, 2020.

15. Isabel Vincent, "Melania Trump's Girl-on-Girl Photos from Racy Shoot Revealed," New York Post, August 1, 2016, https://nypost. com/2016/08/01/melania-trumps-girl-on-girl-photos-from-racy-shootrevealed/, viewed July 4, 2020.

16. Isabel Vincent, "Melania Trump Like You've Never Seen Her Before," New York Post, July 30, 2016, viewed July 4, 2020.

17. David Smith, "Melania Trump in New Plagiarism Row over Online Safety Pamphlet," The Guardian, May 8, 2018. https://www.theguardian.com/us-news/2018/may/07/melania-trump-plagiarism-row-be-best-campaign, viewed July 4, 2020.

18. Mary Jordan, *The Art of Her Deal: The Untold Story of Melania Trump* (New York: Simon and Schuster, 2020), 275.

19. Kate Anderson Brower, "Melania Shows She's a Trump Through and Through," CNN, December 15, 2018. https://www.cnn.com/2018/12/13/opinions/melania-trump-interview-poll-brower/index.html, viewed July 3, 2020.

Chapter Six In All Honesty

1. Marc Thiessen, "Trump Could Be the Most Honest President in Modern History," Washington Post, October 11, 2018, https://www.washingtonpost.com/opinions/trump-could-be-the-most-honest-president-in-modern-history/2018/10/11/67aefc5a-cd76-11e8-a3e6-44daa3d35ede_story.html , viewed July 26, 2020.

2. Donald Trump, *The Art of the Deal* (New York: Ballantine Books, 1987), 58.

3. Donald J. Trump, *Great Again: How to Fix Our Crippled America* (New York: Threshold Editions, 2016), 8–9.

4. Thiessen.

5. Thiessen.

6. Thiessen.

7. Trump, *Great Again*, 7.

8. Thiessen.

9. Trump, *Great Again,* 137.

10. Tammy Bruce, *Varney*, Fox Business Channel, January 31, 2020.

11. Donald Trump, "President Trump Goes One-on-One with Chris Wallace," Fox News, July 19, 2020, https://www.youtube.com/watch?v=W6XdpDOH1JA , viewed July 20, 2020.

12. Gene Ho, *Trumpography: How Biblical Principles Paved the Way to American Presidency* (iUniverse, 2018), 159.

13. Newt Gingrich, *Understanding Trump* (New York: Center Street, 2017), 11.

14. Trump, *The Art of the Deal*, 58.

15. Donald J. Trump, *Think Like a Champion: An Informal Education in Business and Life* (New York: RP Minis, 2010), 32.

16. Gingrich, *Understanding Trump,* 11.

17. Trump, *Think Like a Champion*, xi.

18. David Brody and Scott Lamb, *The Faith of Donald J. Trump* (New York: Broadside Books, 2018), 260.

19. Brody and Lamb, *The Faith of Donald J. Trump*, 260.

20. Trump, *Great Again: How to Fix Our Crippled America,* 132.

Chapter Seven American Original

1. Newt Gingrich, *Understanding Trump* (New York: Center Street, 2017), 4.

2. Gwenda Blair, *The Trumps: Three Generations That Built an Empire* (New York: Simon and Schuster, 2000), 250.

3. Donald J. Trump, *Great Again: How to Fix Our Crippled America* (New York: Threshold Editions, 2015), 99.

4. Blair, *The Trumps*, 251.

5. Gene Ho, *Trumpography: How Biblical Principles Paved the Way to the American Presidency* (iUniverse, 2018), 127.

6. Blair, 231.

7. Blair, 232.

8. Blair, 232–33.

9. Blair, 236.

10. Blair, 237.

11. Blair, 239.

12. Blair, 240.

13. Blair, 242.

14. Blair, 242.

15. Blair, 239.

16. Gingrich, 53.

17. Gingrich, 8.

18. Donald J. Trump, *Think Like a Champion: An Informal Education in Business and Life* (New York: RP Minis, 2010), 49.

19. Trump, *Think Like a Champion*, 49.

20. Donald J. Trump with Meredith McIver, *Trump Never Give Up: How I Turned My Biggest Challenges into Success* (Hoboken, New Jersey: Wiley, 2008), 46.

21. Trump, *Think Like a Champion*, 187.

22. Blair, 271.

23. Blair, 228.

24. Blair, 271.

25. Blair, 260.

26. David Brody and Scott Lamb, *The Faith of Donald J. Trump* (New York: Broadside Books, 2018), 94.

Chapter Eight Master of the Mic

1. Donald J. Trump, *Think Like a Champion: An Informal Education in Business and Life* (New York: RP Minis, 2010), 157.

2. Trump, *Think Like a Champion*, 159.

3. Donald Trump, *The Art of the Deal* (New York: Ballantine Books, 1987), 32.

4. Nancy Benac, "Road to Debate: Trump Built Image as He Built Business," Associated Press, September 26, 2016, https://www.pbs.org/newshour/politics/road-debate-trump-built-image-built-business , viewed August 18, 2020.

5. Benac, "Road to Debate."

6. Benac, "Road to Debate."

7. Susan Mulcahy, "Confessions of a Trump Tabloid Scribe," politico. com, May/June 2016, https://www.politico.com/magazine/story/2016/04/2016-donald-trump-tabloids-new-york-post-daily-news-media-213842, viewed August 20, 2020.

8. The Hollywood Reporter Staff, "Donald Trump's Wife, Children Open Up on '20/20 about GOP Candidate: 'There's No One Else Like Him,'" hollywoodreporter.com, November 21, 2015, https://www.hollywoodreporter.com/news/donald-trumps-wife-children-open-842637, viewed August 20, 2020.

9. Jackie Calmes, "Donald Trump: Life Before the Presidency," millercenter.org, date unknown, https://millercenter.org/president/trump/lifepresidency, viewed August 21, 2020

10. Newt Gingrich, *Understanding Trump* (New York: Center Street, 2017), 87.

11. Gingrich, *Understanding Trump*, 87.

12. Trump, *Think Like a Champion*, 107.

13. Benac.

14. David Brody and Scott Lamb, *The Faith of Donald J. Trump* (New York: Broadside Books, 2018), 82.

15. Brody and Lamb, *The Faith of Donald J. Trump*, 185.

16. Brody and Lamb, 175.

17. Lauren Katz, "Trump Rallies Aren't a Sideshow—They're His Entire Campaign," vox.com, November 6, 2019, https://www.vox.com/policy-and-politics/2019/11/6/20950388/donald-trump-rally-2020-presidential-election-today-explained , viewed August 22, 2020.

18. Donald J. Trump, *Great Again: How to Fix Our Crippled America* (New York: Threshold Editions, 2015), 10–11.

19. Newt Gingrich, Trump's America (New York: Center Street, 2018), 192.

20. Gingrich, *Understanding Trump*, 18.

21. Brody and Lamb, 147.

Chapter Nine Take the Lead

1. Medically reviewed by Julie Dodson, "What is the Childhood of a Leader Personality Type Like?", betterhelp.com, updated February 25, 2024. https://www.betterhelp.com/advice/childhood/what-is-the-childhood-of-a-leader/ , viewed March 21, 2024.

2. Krystine I. Batcho PH.D., "Childhood Happiness: More Than Just Child's Play," psychologytoday.com, Jan. 13, 2012 https://www.psychologytoday.com/us/blog/longing-nostalgia/201201/childhood-happiness-more-just-childs-play, viewed February 7, 2024.

3. W. Bradford Wilcox, David Bass, "Growing Up in Intact Families Matters More Than Ever," aei.org, October 2, 2023, https://www.aei.org/articles/growing-up-in-intact-families-matters-more-than-ever/, viewed February 7, 2024.

4. Donald J. Trump with Meredith McIver, *Trump Never Give Up: How I Turned My Biggest Challenges into Success* (Hoboken, NJ: Wiley, 2008), 19.

5. Gwenda Blair, *The Trumps: Three Generations That Built an Empire* (New York: Simon and Schuster, 2000), 224.

6. Blair, *The Trumps*, 230.

7. Blair, 230.

8. Blair, 230.

9. Donald Trump, *The Art of the Deal* (New York: Ballantine Books, 1987), 72.

10. Donald J. Trump, *Think Like a Champion: An Informal Education in Business and Life* (New York: RP Minis, 2010), 70.

11. Donald Trump, *The Art of the Deal* (New York: Ballantine Books, 1987), 89.

12. Newt Gingrich, *Understanding Trump* (New York: Center Street, 2017), 73.

13. David Brody and Scott Lamb, *The Faith of Donald J. Trump* (New York: Broadside Books, 2018), 74.

14. Brody and Lamb, 286.

15. Michael D'Antonio, *Never Enough: Donald Trump and the Pursuit of Success* (New York, New York: Thomas Dunne Books, 2015), 47.

16. Trump, *Think Like a Champion*, 181.

17. Trump, *Think Like a Champion*, 25.

18. Trump, *Think Like a Champion*, 182.

19. Trump, *The Art of the Deal*, 140.

20. Phillips, *Lincoln on Leadership: Executive Strategies for Tough Times*, 135.

21. https://transparency.kununu.com/compelling-qualities-of-greatleaders/, viewed October 16, 2020.

22. https://transparency.kununu.com/compelling-qualities-of-great-leaders/ .

23. Edward Achorn, *Every Drop of Blood: The Momentous Second Inauguration of Abraham Lincoln* (New York: Atlantic Monthly Press, 2020), first page of chapter 3 (page number unknown).

24. Goodwin, 235.

25. Newt Gingrich, *Understanding Trump* (New York: Center Street, 2017), xvi.

26. Donald J. Trump, *Great Again: How to Fix Our Crippled America* (New York: Threshold Editions, 2015) 3.

27. https://transparency.kununu.com/compelling-qualities-of-greatleaders/ ,viewed October 17, 2020.

28. Gingrich, *Understanding Trump,* 15.

29. Donald, *Think Like a Champion: An Informal Education in Business and Life,* 29.

30. Donald, *The Art of the Deal,* 140.

Chapter Ten A House Divided

1. Newt Gingrich, *Understanding Trump* (New York: Center Street, 2017), 164.

2. Newt Gingrich, *Trump's America* (New York: Center Street, 2018), 187.

3. Gingrich, *Understanding Trump,* 164.

4. David Herbert Donald, *Lincoln* (New York: Simon and Schuster, 1996), 80.

5. Edward Achorn, "24 Tense Hours in Abraham Lincoln's Life," New York Times, February 23, 2020, https://zukus.net/2020/02/24-tense-hoursin-abraham-lincolns-life/# , viewed October 28, 2020.

6. Gingrich, *Understanding Trump,* 165.

7. Leonard L. Richards, *Who Freed the Slaves?: The Fight over the Thirteenth Amendment* (Chicago and London: The University of Chicago Press, 2015), 170.

8. Donald T. Phillips, *Lincoln on Leadership: Executive Strategies for Tough Times* (New York: Warner Books, 1993), 173.

9. Gingrich, *Trump's America,* 3.

10. Gingrich, *Understanding Trump,* 150.

11. Gingrich, *Understanding Trump,* 150–51, 160.

12. Lincoln, Abraham, and Roy P. Basler, ed. *The Collected Works of Abraham Lincoln, 9th edition.* (New Brunswick, NJ: Rutgers University Press, 1953), volume 4, 160.

13. Gingrich, *Understanding Trump,* 141.

14. Gingrich, *Understanding Trump*, 141–42.

15. Gingrich, *Understanding Trump*, 99.

16. Gingrich, *Understanding Trump*, 146.

17. Gingrich, *Understanding Trump*, 151.

18. Dinesh D'Souza, *Death of a Nation: Plantation Politics and the Making of the Democratic Party* (New York: All Points Books, 2018), xiii.

19. D'Souza, *Death of a Nation*, xiii.

20. D'Souza, xv.

21. D'Souza, xvi.

22. D'Souza, 53.

23. D'Souza, 53, 55.

24. D'Souza, 25.

25. Phillips, *Lincoln on Leadership for Today*, 82.

26. D'Souza, 91.

27. D'Souza, 91.

28. "Summary of Election Fraud in the 2020 Presidential Election in the Swing States" https://cdn. nucleusfiles.com/e0/e04e630c-63ff-4bdb-9652-e0be3598b5d4s ummary20of20election20fraud 20in20the20swing20states.pdf

29. D'Souza, 277.

30. D'Souza, 276.

Bibliography

Abraham Lincoln, His Words and His World. New York: Country Beautiful Foundation for Hawthorn Books, 1965.

Abrams, Dan, and David Fisher. *Lincoln's Last Trial: The Murder Case That Propelled Him to the Presidency.* New York: Hanover Square Press, 2018.

Achorn, Edward. *Every Drop of Blood: The Momentous Second Inauguration of Abraham Lincoln.* New York: Atlantic Monthly Press, 2020.

Blair, Gwenda. *The Trumps: Three Generations That Built an Empire.* New York: Simon & Schuster, 2000.

Blaisdell, Bob ed. *The Wit and Wisdom of Abraham Lincoln: A Book of Quotations.* Mineola, NY: Dover Publications, 2005.

Brody, David and Scott Lamb. *The Faith of Donald J. Trump.* New York: Broadside Books, 2018.

D'Antonio, Michael. *Never Enough: Donald Trump and the Pursuit of Success.* New York: Thomas Dunne Books, 2015.

Donald, David Herbert. *Lincoln.* New York: Simon and Schuster, 1996.

D'Souza, Dinesh. *Death of a Nation: Plantation Politics and the Making of the Democratic Party.* New York: All Points Books, 2018.

Freehling, William W. *Becoming Lincoln.* Charlottesville, VA: University of Virginia Press, 2018.

Gingrich, Newt. *Trump's America*. New York: Center Street, 2018.

Gingrich, Newt. *Understanding Trump*. New York: Center Street, 2017.

Goodwin, Doris Kearns. *Team of Rivals: The Political Genius of Abraham Lincoln*. New York: Simon & Schuster paperbacks, 2005.

Herndon, William H., *Herndon's Lincoln: The True Story of a Great Life*, paperback. CreateSpace Independent Publishing Platform, 2014.

Herndon, William H. *The Hidden Lincoln: From the Letters and Papers of William H. Herndon*. London: Forgotten Books, 2018.

Ho, Gene. *Trumpography: How Biblical Principles Paved the Way to the American Presidency*. iUniverse, 2018.

Jordan, Mary. *The Art of Her Deal: The Untold Story of Melania Trump*. New York: Simon and Schuster, 2020.

Kouwenhoven, John A. *Adventures of America: 1857–1900: A Pictorial Record from Harper's Weekly*. New York and London: Harper & Brothers Publishers, 1938.

Lincoln, Abraham, and Roy P. Basler, ed. *The Collected Works of Abraham Lincoln, 9th edition*. The Abraham Lincoln Association, Springfield, IL. New Brunswick, NJ: Rutgers University Press, 1953.

Ludwig, Emil. *Abraham Lincoln and the Times that Tried His Soul*. New York: Fawcett Publications, 1956.

McPherson, James. *Tried by War: Abraham Lincoln as Commander in Chief*. New York: Penguin Books, 2009.

Medved, Michael. *God's Hand on America: Divine Providence in the Modern Era*. New York: Crown Forum, 2019.

National Geographic Society. *We Americans*. Washington, D.C: National Geographic Society, 1988.

O'Reilly, Bill. *The United States of Trump: How the President Really Sees America*. New York: Henry Holt and Company, 2019.

Peraino, Kevin. *Lincoln in the World: The Making of a Statesman and the Dawn of American Power*. New York: Broadway Books, 2014.

Phillips, Donald T. *Lincoln on Leadership: Executive Strategies for Tough Times*. New York: Warner Books, 1993.

Phillips, Donald T. *Lincoln on Leadership for Today: Abraham Lincoln's Approach to Twenty-First Century Issues.* Boston, MA: Mariner Books, 2017.

Polley, Robert L., ed. *Lincoln: His Words and His World.* Waukesha, WI: Country Beautiful Foundation, 1965.

Richards, Leonard L. *Who Freed the Slaves?: The Fight over the Thirteenth Amendment.* Chicago and London: The University of Chicago Press, 2015.

Trump, Donald J., with Kate Bohner. *The Art of the Comeback.* New York: Times Books, 1997.

Trump, Donald. *The Art of the Deal.* New York: Ballantine Books, 1987.

Trump, Donald J. *Great Again: How to Fix Our Crippled America.* New York: Threshold Editions, 2015.

Trump, Donald J. *Time to Get Tough: Making America #1 Again.* Washington DC: Regnery Publishing, Inc. 2011.

Trump, Donald J., with Meredith McIver. *Trump: Never Give Up: How I Turned My Biggest Challenges into Success.* Hoboken, NJ: Wiley, 2008.

Trump, Ivana. *Raising Trump.* New York: Gallery Books, 2017.

About the Author

Teacher, entrepreneur, farmer, rancher, author—Gretchen Wollert has worn many hats. She continues to actively influence others toward truth in American history and politics with her first comparative biography *Born to Fight: Lincoln & Trump*, and now with her new strategic excerpt *The Magic & Mayhem of Donald Trump*. Degrees in English and history, and her professional expertise in education compliment her extensive experience in the field of hard work. Extremely active in life and adventurous to a fault, Gretchen is a forever fan of family, faith, and freedom. Devoted to a growing extended family of four grown daughters, sons-in-law, and ever-increasing grandchildren, Gretchen lives and works with her husband Mike just off the beaten path in Southeast Wyoming.